NEVER
EVER GIVE UP

FREDRICK

NEVER EVER GIVE UP

LIFE AND LESSONS

THINGS WORK OUT IN THE END, IF THEY DON'T, IT'S NOT THE END!

J. STANLEY FREDRICK

Clovercroft Publishing

Never Ever Give Up: Life and Lessons

© 2022 by Stan Fredrick

Published by Clovercroft Publishing, Franklin, Tennessee

Edited by Adept Content Solutions and Results Faster

Cover design by Debbie Manning Sheppard

Interior design by Adept Content Solutions

Printed in the United States of America

978-1-954437-04-3

Most Results Faster! Publishing books are available in special quantity discounts when purchased in bulk by corporations, organizations, and special interest groups. Custom imprinting or excerpting can also be done to fit special needs. For information, please call (817) 430-9422.

FREDRICK

CONTENTS

ƒ FREDRICK ƒ

DEDICATED TO JOHN FREDRICK

Brothers: Stan and John Fredrick as they appear

To my older brother John who always introduced me as his partner, saying we had been together all my life and most of his. We lost John in January of 2017. We had been partners for over three-quarters of a century. Even though I was three years younger, he always included me in everything he did or tried. Mom and Dad always figured I was safe if I was with John. It was common for us as five- and eight-year old's to walk to the creek 7 miles from the house to cool off in the limestone pools, ride double on his bike to school, and even go on dates when he was old enough. When it comes to work, we spaded up gardens together, teamed up to mow lawns, got paper routes together, and went on the road to sell pots and pans when I was just 16 years old. Looking back, I realized now he was teaching and training me so that one day I could be his equal and pull my share of the load as we built a legacy for the Fredrick family that would live on after we were gone. Although I never felt quite his equal, I was able to fill in for him on things he didn't like to do, find opportunities that allowed us to grow Cameo even bigger, introduce him to the investment side of banking, and together we built a ranch that fulfilled our greatest dream. When it was time for him to slow down, he encouraged me to forge ahead on my own with Mannatech and Wine Shop. He celebrated our achievements, lamented with me our setbacks, yet always expressing optimism for the future. We enjoyed his final years together, reliving the past, enjoying the present and planning the future. I dedicate this book to John because I know that it was his faith in me, his loving loyalty and his inspiring strength that drove my mantra to never ever give up.

ƒ FREDRICK ƒ

ACKNOWLEDGMENTS

To Kristin Birdwell for her patient shepherding of this writing process. She transcribed my Texas colloquialisms and my stream of conciousness ramblings, and logically linked the varied dreams, actions, activities and emotions that comprised my life.

To Tony Jeary whom I have worked with for the past decade as a coach, strategic planning leader, mentor, and friend, and now as my publisher, who believed I had a story worth publishing and encouraged me to tell it.

To my big, beautiful family, and especially my wife Judy, who have been with me through the ups and downs, helping make all my dreams come true. I am very thankful for them putting up with me and encouraging me in the writing of this book.

To all the present and past DSA Board of director members who were kind and patient to this fellow board member who consistently questioned and challenged anything he felt did not appear to be in the best interest of this great Direct-Selling Industry. You ultimately helped shape him, his life, and business. Thank you.

To all the past, present and future employees and associates of Mannatech whose belief, courage and persistence made Mannatech's mission and vision a reality and helping make my story worth telling.

To Ella Imrie for her charming yet professional way of keeping us all working together and to all the team at RESULTS Faster Publishing, for getting the document written, edited, and turned into a book.

To all of the friends, partners, customers, and distributors who have believed in me, coached me, taught me, while inspiring me to never ever give up.

FREDRICK

INTRODUCTION

"Every achievement of man is a value in itself, but it is also a stepping-stone to greater achievements and values. Life is growth; not to move forward, is to fall backward; life remains life, only so long as it advances. ...Achievement is man's highest moral purpose."
Ayn Rand

The Direct Selling News Lifetime Achievement Award—how did I get here? And where do I go from this point? While John Fleming detailed some of my achievements within the industry, I stood behind the curtain and reflected on the events leading up to this moment. *Direct Selling News* was envisioned and created by Stuart Johnson and built into the premier publication of the direct-selling industry by John Fleming, its editor and publisher. *Direct Selling News* created this Lifetime Achievement Award, and I was honored to be the second person to receive it. Even the simple fact that I was about to walk onto the stage was an incredible feat. Over the previous year, I'd spent nine months between a hospital and a physical therapy rehabilitation center battling sepsis, colon cancer, and a hip replacement. So you could certainly say my life had comprised challenges and successes—often in that order.

Being the second person to receive the award was a huge honor, and although I knew I'd achieved more than a lot of people had, a part of me didn't feel worthy of this kind of distinction. My stint in the hospital had given me time for quite the life review, showing me how fortunate I'd been to have accomplished what I had. It was the result of unrelenting persistence and my propensity to take advantage of opportunities, but it was also the result of partnering with others, their contributions, and of conjunctions of circumstances and events.

For a boy from a poor family, receiving the Direct Selling News Lifetime Achievement Award was almost unbelievable. I had been lucky to encounter the direct-selling industry, and now my history of direct selling spanned more than six decades and three careers. I'd advocated for the direct-selling industry for more than forty years, based on my belief in the industry's power to help a lot of people grow and achieve.

> I'd advocated for the direct-selling industry for more than forty years, based on my belief in the industry's power to help a lot of people.

In the late 1930s, just shy of two years old, I'd bumped up and down in a steel-wheeled wagon, seated beside my mom. Her eyes squinted as she stared forward, carefully guiding the mules in a straight line through the cornfield. My dad and extended family members pulled the corn and tossed it in the back of the wagon—everyone turned out to help. I grew up seeing people work hard and understanding that work was a part of life and nothing to be afraid of, no matter a person's history or station in life. I understand now how my parents' influence, particularly in that moment, modeled the way in which partnering as a team ultimately reaps the harvest. They taught me that it takes a lot of people to help one person succeed.

My parents' work ethic and the lessons they taught me helped build my persistence. I don't quit, and I've never understood quitting. Over the years, even in the hospital, when I was unable to talk or convey my thoughts, I returned to what my father had taught me in childhood: *Get back on the horse. Get back up one more time. Keep going, and hold on to the belief that things will work out in the end—and that if they aren't working out right now, then it's not the end.*

I always felt like being an English teacher or professor would give me a chance to help students experience the joy, growth, and inspiration I received from Dad talking about the novels he'd read or listening to him read his favorite poems such as "The Raven," "The Psalm of Life," "Invictus," or of his favorite Bible scriptures, such as "As a man thinketh in his heart so is he."

Even though I decided not to be a literature professor, I used my love of the written word as an opportunity to pepper my teaching, preaching, and speeches with quotations and poems that have inspired me. You will find some of them that had special impact on my life or touched me in this story. Poems were a favorite way of evoking a scene or describing emotions during the ups and downs of my life, so I have included them as they occurred along the way

Maybe it was the combination of luck and persistence that led to my bit of success and my receipt of that award. Yet, despite having achieved nearly everything I'd ever dreamed of: a beautiful, incredible wife, five great kids, a thousand-acre ranch, a condo in Hawaii, a sailing adventure in the British Virgin Islands, big game hunting, helping people learn more and live happier lives, and enough money in the bank to never have to work again, I still felt more needed to be done. I know now that a lot of that feeling stemmed from my desire to ensure that my legacy was perpetual; I wanted to make sure there was something left over after I was gone, and I've been working on that ever since. Part of that work has included passing on the businesses that are designed to do what I could not do in a classroom: help thousands of people develop and prosper, nourish starving kids, honoring and supporting veterans and gold star families, and passing on the fruits of my life's harvest. Another part has been sharing my story—compiling the lessons, strategies, and philosophies I've picked up along the way into this book so I can help others achieve their goals.

I have always been more of a behind-the-scenes guy. Yet after a little encouraging nudge from successful publisher, Tony Jeary, who'd also helped us with strategic planning at Independent National Bank and Mannatech, I decided to consider the idea of telling my story. Being on the telling side of

Another part has been sharing my story–compiling the lessons, strategies, and philosophies I've picked up along the way into this book so I can help others achieve their goals.

the story is a bit foreign for me; however, in the following pages, I hope to share with you the *aha!* moments I've had in my life while expressing my appreciation for the people who helped inspire them, thereby contributing to my achievements.

So I invite you to join me on the journey from graduating high school at sixteen years old with ten dollars in my pocket to operating multimillion-dollar direct-sales companies that span the globe. Through stories, insights, and an occasional poem, we'll discover what factors and feelings helped me succeed—and how you may use them to build on your success.

NEVER EVER GIVE UP

CHAPTER 1

BRAINSTORMING OUR FIRST ENTERPRISING ADVENTURE

*"Far away there in the sunshine are my highest aspirations.
I may not reach them, but I can look up and see their beauty,
believe in them, and try to follow where they lead."*
Louisa May Alcott

I've always enjoyed building and designing things. My first venture into manufacture and design came in the third grade after our move to Dallas. My older brother John's fifth-grade teacher had assigned the kids to make hot-pad holders, a project involving sanding plywood squares, shellacking the wood, and adding a little rose decal. We added cup hooks into three corners and drilled a hole in the other corner to hang it by. When John gave the finished product to Mom on Mother's Day, her excitement about the gift spurred our first enterprising adventure.

We brainstormed ways of making and selling a similar item, walked to the grocery store, and found a couple discarded apple crates for our new project. We took the ends off the twenty-four by twenty-four-inch crates, sawed them into six-inch squares, sanded and shellacked them, then added a decal and hooks, and sold them all for twenty-five cents apiece.

I don't know why we didn't make any more after selling out our stock, but I understand the value in that experience today, and it's convinced me that experience is the best school; to live it is to get it. Even if you can't see or pinpoint the reasoning at the time, each moment prepares you for the next—or for a time later in life. As Mark Twain said, "If a cat sits on a hot stove, it will never sit on a hot stove again. Of course, that cat won't sit on a cold one, either." This moment in design, manufacturing, and sales prepped John and me for the experiences and challenges in the years to come.

Strategy: Be Careful What You Feed Your Mind

As an eight-year-old boy, I'd lived half my life in Waco. We lived in an old farmhouse, split so two families could live there, with a living room, a bedroom, a kitchen, and a screened-in back porch where John and I slept during scorching summers and freezing winters. The porch was just big enough to have a twin-sized bed. Several times the snow came in and covered the blankets over us.

Experience is the best school; to live it is to get it. Even if you can't see or pinpoint the reasoning at the time, each moment prepares you for the next–or for a time later in life.

Dad was working for the government by then, but the pay was low for beginners. So yes—we were poor; but I didn't know that until I was in a little country store about a half-mile down the road from our house. I'd gone to buy a loaf of bread, and as I was leaving, the store owner responded to someone's inquiry about me by saying, "Oh, that's one of the poor Fredrick boys." *Poor?* I'd never thought about that. I stood outside, shirtless, and looked down at the homemade shorts and my bare feet before

I started walking down the dirt road back home. The word stuck in my head. *Okay, I'm poor?* I did not know for sure what it meant. I just knew I never wanted people to look at me like that.

A short time later, I found out how the mind controls our body and our emotions in a subtle way. I was playing out in the front yard with a bumblebee on my finger. People tend to fear them because of their ferocious sting, but there I was, sitting and playing with one and letting it crawl around my fingers. I'd been playing with it for some time when Mom came out, saw it, and said, "Oh, get away from there. That'll sting you." The bumblebee immediately stung me. I've thought many times about that scenario—about how her saying those words triggered something in me that made me afraid, and in response, the bee stung me. I realized then how powerful the mind is and how it accepts influence from other people—how we need to be careful about what goes in our head, what we say, and what we accept from others. Now, I realize the mind can control a bumblebee's stinger if it doesn't react to voices of fear.

Ashly, fourth child and third daughter,

"Dad knows there is power in words. When raising my kids, my youngest, Brandon, was climbing on the jungle gym in the backyard. I was talking to Dad on the phone when Brandon started walking across the top of one of those old silver galvanized posts with his arms out to balance. I said, "Brandon, stop. You could fall."

"Ashly," Dad said. "Don't say that to him."

"I was telling him to be careful."

"Actually," he said. "You just told him he *could* fall."

In that moment, he taught me that when you're voicing something, you've got to watch the words that you speak for yourself and others. Words have meaning and impact."

Lesson: There Is Power in Visualization

Mom made our clothes, and Dad made us dream. He may have not agreed with Roosevelt's politics, but he believed with FDR that the future belonged to those who believed in their dreams. Dad liked the scripture,

"As a man thinketh in his heart so is he." Without aspirations in your heart, you will never grow. Without dreams, life is dull. We needed to say yes to our dreams, and Dad made sure we didn't let our poverty prevent us from dreaming big.

During those days, bluebonnets blanketed the fields in the spring. I laid in the field across the dirt road from my house as if I were about to make a snow angel out of season. I smelled the fragrance, saw their beauty, and gazed into the sky at the billowing clouds as they passed. I dreamed about what those clouds were and what it would be like to float in them, then resolved that one day I'd go up there, touch those clouds, and do whatever I wanted to do. Later when I read Louisa May Alcott's words, "Somewhere up there in the sunshine are my highest aspirations, I may not reach them, but I will follow them wherever they lead," I would come to learn that to achieve something great, we must first imagine it.

Without aspirations in your heart, you will never grow. Without dreams, life is dull.

During the late 1940s, my brother Craig was born, and my family moved from the farmlands of Waco to Dallas, Texas. Within walking distance of our new home was a little five-and-dime store with a Daisy Red Ryder BB gun hanging in the display window. John, three years my elder, gazed at that gun with me in doe-eyed wonder from the other side of the glass.

It was a replica of the Model 94 Winchester 30–30 Dad had recently bought from a co-worker who had to sell it. He was really excited about getting a gun again since he hunted when he was a kid to put meat on the table. We watched him clean the barrel and polish the stock with loving care. This was the beginning of my love for guns and hunting, and my fascination with that BB gun. That Model 94 was the gun I would use to shoot my first buck. Yet, it would be many years before I would get to go big game hunting in Montana and Colorado.

Every time we went to buy groceries or a loaf of bread, we looked at that gun. Sometimes the owner let us take it down and dream. I turned the gun over in my hands, ran my fingers along the little hanging strip of rawhide, and smelled the leather and wooden stock while envisioning BBs shooting out the end. Holding on to that gun, priced at $4.95, I couldn't imagine having that much money. John and I had once found a nickel and asked Mom whether we could use it to buy a Coke, but we had needed the nickel for a loaf of bread that week.

So with a contagious entrepreneurial spirit, we pushed a lawnmower to mow lawns, starting our next business venture at the same time. One afternoon while sitting on the freshly cut grass, shortly after our first customer had placed two quarters into my brother's sweaty palm, I wiped a bit of sweat from my forehead with a handkerchief and said, "If we mow ten lawns, we could have that Daisy Red Ryder BB gun."

"You know; you're right," he said.

We jumped up and started scouting for lawns to mow, and within a month, we'd earned enough money to go down to the five-and-dime and put that money on the table. That was also the first time I experienced division of efforts and reframed my mind-set. Instead of thinking about how much money I needed to purchase an item, **I began thinking in terms of how many lawns to mow, papers to throw, how many people to talk to or demonstrations to make were necessary to obtain what I wanted.** Yet it all starts with dreams as reflected in this poem.

Reflections, 1958 Poetry Contest Winner

The hungry fire gulped the wooded hearth,
Trees bowed as snow drifted to earth,
Heated flames chased cold from the room,
But a chill in my soul prophesied doom.
Memories stirred in my foggy old brain,
Reality retreated, youth caressed me again.
To childhood's Christmas Eve again I went,
Eighty years, a speck of time, have been spent.
I ran to my mother, a boy of eight,
Hugged her tight, asked if Santa'd be late,
Kissed and assured, I made my retreat,
Raised on toes when cold burned my feet.

Reluctance undressed me casually at first,
But then like a flash as joy in me burst,
Mother had said, "If I'd hurry to bed,
Santa'd come sooner with toys in his sled."
I climbed the wall-ladder to the chilled loft,
Smoothed the straw and shucks, shivered, and coughed.
Over the side, I saw the tree below,
Visioned my gifts that flew over the snow.
Dreaming my dreams—guns, a horse, and sleigh,
Drifted off in darkness as the fire died away.
Reality seeps back with growing coldness,
The dying fire, darkness comes with boldness,
A serene mind, glowing coals, atmosphere iced,
I will sleep now, maybe forever … "My Christ."

Stan Fredrick

Shortly after our lawn-mowing enterprise, our family moved to the small town of Irving, population 2,400. I began to experience the difference between the haves and have-nots. After school, kids gathered at the Big State Drugstore for a Cherry Coke—some could even afford an ice-cream soda. I sat and talked to kids like Gilbert Porter, Chaney Anderson, and Billy Dearing who would be friends all through school. Mainly listening, feeling completely left out while drinking a free glass of water, I dreamed of better times.

To achieve something great, we must first imagine it.

John had started throwing papers for the *Irving News-Record.* Once a week, he loaded his bag, got on his bike, and went to throw papers. John's reputation reached *The Dallas Morning News,* and they approached him about circulating their paper in Irving. When he asked me whether I wanted to get a paper route and make some money, I jumped at the chance, forgetting for the moment that it meant getting up at 3:00 a.m.

to roll papers and throw them before 5:30 a.m., when people woke up. He negotiated a route for me; so, we became the first and second "paper boys" in Irving.

My first dream came crashing down when I filled the bag, which hung from the handlebars and rested on the fender, and I realized I was too small. The bag was too heavy for me to get my bike going and get on, but John rescued me and held the bike while I got on. He then gave me a push, and off I went on my fifteen-mile route through the outskirts of Irving. Going to bed early and getting up at 3:00 a.m. was rough, but the first time I sat down at that drugstore, ordered a soda, and paid for it with my own money, I knew it had been worth it.

My dreams seemed to come to an end one morning after the first big snowfall. I heard a car coming up behind me and started moving over to the side of the road, but I slipped and fell, and the car hit me. The driver left me beside the road unconscious from a blow to my head, but passersby picked me up and took me to the clinic, where they called one of two doctors in town. They called my parents, who arrived about the same time the doctor did. Dad was so mad, I thought he'd make me give up my route, but I later found out he was upset because the doctor wasn't treating me gently. My clothes were ragged, and I thought the doctor didn't want to deal with poor people. But after Dad straightened him out, he put in a nice set of stitches and sewed up my head.

Stan on his paper route

Our innovative ideas continued throughout those bicycle days. Back then, when somebody rode on your bike with you, we called it pumping since you had to stand on the pedals and push hard. Usually people would sit on the bar, between the cyclist and the handlebars, but when we emptied that bag, we found we could sit on the handlebars and lean back on the strap that went behind us for a snooze. So John and I traded out, with one of us riding and taking a little nap while the other one did the pumping. That taught me **the power of people partnering together**—you gain momentum in life and share the rewards, as I would see again later in direct sales.

Managing the newspaper route was my first independent sales contractor job. The real cherries on top of the five-year experience as a paperboy were the key business elements learned: discipline (getting up at 3:00 a.m.), courage (knocking on strangers' doors), and finance (collecting money and paying the bill for the papers thrown the month before.)

The power of people partnering together—you gain momentum in life and share the rewards.

Strategy: Leverage the Power of Persistence

One serendipitous summer, Dad took the whole family to my uncle's farm. He had been raised on a horse, so riding came naturally, but this was the first time I'd ridden one. It was a registered quarter horse with the most beautiful foxtrot you've ever seen—a ride so comfortable it was like sitting in a rocking chair. When I started riding him, he just clomped along, but when I bounced up to Dad, he said, "That horse is trained to foxtrot. Now, you take off and make him foxtrot. And don't you come back until you have him trotting."

I was scared to death but took off. I don't know how, or whether the horse heard Dad or what, but somehow I got that horse to foxtrot. My dad's hand and hoof lesson in perseverance, in never giving up, was part of the discipline that helped my brother and me make strides later in life.

After that lesson, I won my first contest shortly after. The *Dallas Morning News* ran a contest for the paper boys who sold the most new subscriptions. I still don't know if it was the recognition or the winning trip to the Shangri La Dude Ranch that inspired me. One of the highlights of that trip was the horseback riding. When the wrangler asked if anyone knew how to ride, I felt a sense of pride in being the only one putting up a hand. Truth be told, my only experience was that successful ride making my uncle's horse Buck foxtrot. A little fear crept in when he said, "Well good, you can ride this spirited stallion."

Well, I did just fine … as would seem to be the case for other challenges life presented.

Besides, the horse never knew it was just my second time.

Stan on 'Buck' the Registered Quarter Horse

Julie, first child

"Dad is one of the most courageous and bravest people I know. He taught us that if you don't do things that you're afraid of, you'll never move forward. Later in life, Dad told me when he didn't know how to do this or didn't know how to do that, he studied, learned, and read. You learn so you can move forward and grow."

Lesson: Act Before You're Perfectly Ready

In high school, amid the heartbreak of not lettering for football and seeing John leave for college, I shifted my focus to my school studies so I could graduate early. Dad had always told us that we had to attend college, but he hadn't told us how to pay for it. So when John got there, he found out he'd have to work to make the money to pay for college. Then he got a card in the mail that read "How would you like to earn fifty dollars a week working part-time?"

Needless to say, he answered the ad and found it was selling waterless cookware to single girls. He caught the direct-selling fever with VitaCraft, a manufacturer of aluminum pots and pans. I didn't know it then, but soon I'd have the fever, too.

While Dad was working for the government, we had our first official experience with direct selling. He'd taken a part-time job selling with WearEver, and for a year or two, he cooked dinners at people's homes to help our family out of a little financial bind and pay for our recent house purchase. Dad was among the first distributors to demonstrate WearEver's new line of Cutco knives. When I later told Eric Lane, the owner of Cutco and a DSA board member, about being among the first owners of Cutco knives, we bonded immediately.

During the first summer John worked, he kept coming home and telling me how well he was doing. I was staggered by how much a kid could make selling on commission. At that time, we worked on a 25 percent commission structure, which meant when you sold a cookware set for $148.05, a whopping $37 of it went in your wallet. You could earn more than a full week's wages in about an hour and a half.

When I graduated at sixteen, I had ten dollars in my pocket and John's voice in my ear, nudging me to join his pots-and-pans venture. Having witnessed Dad's experience in the industry, hearing about John's money-making experience, and imagining selling to single girls made me quite receptive to the idea. That's not to say I didn't have my doubts. I did not have a car, was not successful with women, did not know how to sell, and did not have money for expenses. John responded with a solution that helped me make up my mind.

"I'll show you how to sell," he said. "I can drop you off at appointments until you get a car. And you have the $10 you got for graduation."

So on the way from Irving to Houston for a training session, John gave me a fast-track tutorial for selling to single, working girls looking to add to their hope chest, which in those days was where single women collected special items in anticipation of marriage. After John and I piled into a big old house we rented with twenty other salesmen, we went downtown one sunny afternoon in Beaumont to prospect. John spotted two women walking down the street and shoved me out of the car and into the street to sell. I certainly didn't feel ready, even though I'd memorized the typical sales pitch, which opened with *"Pardon me, my name is Stan Fredrick—I wonder if you could help me a minute? I'm going to go to school at Abilene Christian and working here for the summer."* But as I ran to catch up with those two ladies, memorization gave way to nerves, and I lost the words somewhere on the sidewalk.

Heart racing like a thoroughbred, I approached them from behind and nervously asked, "Pardon me, are you girls married?"

One of the women glanced down at her protruding belly—she was probably pushing nine months pregnant—and said, "Well, if I'm not, I ought to be."

They both laughed good naturedly. Then her kind friend took a liking to me and nudged me along the process. She said, "I'm not married. What are you selling?"

"Cookware for your hope chest."

"I'd like to see them," she said.

"Great," I said and turned around to leave.

She asked, "Don't you want to know when?"

"Oh, yes—how about this evening?"

"Sure, wanna tell me what time?"

Later that evening, after my brother dropped me off at the woman's home, I began the presentation and spread out twenty-one pieces of pots and pans from the suitcase, then sat down beside her with an order pad to take her through the nine-point close.

I was so nervous that when she'd signed the order, I forgot step four, to ask for the deposit. She asked, "Don't you want a down payment?"

"Yes, ma'am," I said. "I forgot, do you want to get that for me?"

"You take a check?" she asked.

That woman essentially walked me through my entire first direct-sales experience. Afterward, she even kneeled down and helped me repack the suitcase—you had to place the cookware inside just so or it wouldn't fit.

With her helpful nature, my confidence grew, and I continued walking the street, talking to girls, and making appointments. In a little over two weeks, I had paid all my expenses and had enough money left over to buy a used 1947 Ford. If I'd waited until I felt a hundred percent ready, I'd probably still be on the street in Beaumont. I have often wondered if that woman in Beaumont had any idea of the impact she had on my life and thousands of others.

I've been fortunate enough to have had three distinct careers in direct selling: twenty years in the cookware business, twenty-five years in the lingerie party business, and almost twenty years in the nutrition and network marketing business. All three were crucial to my growth as a businessman and as an individual. A combination of chance encounters, kindness, luck, and persistence influenced my careers—but I've also discovered that the more persistent you are, the luckier you get.

That freshman year, I had enough money left from the summer to pay my way. I spent more time studying than really getting out and working hard, but then I found out that if you don't make a lot of demonstrations and you don't see a lot of people, you're done—you just won't be successful.

By the time Christmas rolled around, I'd been turned down so much I felt as if I couldn't sell any more; I thought I must have gotten lucky that first summer because, based on my recent track record, there was no way I was a good salesman. So when VitaCraft called everyone to meet and sell between Christmas and the new year, I said, "*Not me—I'm not going to do that.*"

A combination of chance encounters, kindness, luck, and persistence influenced my careers–but I've also discovered that the more persistent you are, the luckier you get.

Instead, a friend of ours with a construction company agreed to let me work for him over the holidays. So I went down to the site on Monday morning at eight o'clock. When I arrived, he pointed to a pile of wood and said, "Stan, you see that stack of sixteen-foot two-by-fours? I need them up on the second floor of this building. There's a ladder. Just take the boards up there."

When I lifted that first one, I thought *Okay—I can do this,* and I carried them up. I started carrying them two at a time, but boy, by the time that stack had dwindled, I'd gone back to carrying one again, and I realized I had never worked so hard for so little. I was making minimum wage, about seventy-five cents an hour, which was equivalent to thirty dollars a week. I still haven't forgotten the feel of that lumber on my shoulder. It was such brutal, back-breaking work. After I finished, knocking on doors seemed to be an easier way to make money. I wrote the following poem during a slump that first summer.

The Salesman

Stan Fredrick

I push myself into the street;
Like a salesman should, I pound my beat.
Working hard for at least a minute,
I've made no money but still I've spent it.
As the sweat pouts down my overworked head,
a little voice calls me back to my bed.
Sound asleep at my lush motel,
My dreams are disturbed by the sound of a bell.
The longing, lurking landlord lumbers in;
By the scowl on his face, he could bite through tin.
The rent is due, I've nothing to barter.
The little voice lied—I should've worked harder.

Lesson: Invest Energy in Time Blocking and Scheduling

So in spring 1956, with John as my manager, I started recruiting and developing people for a team training and kickoff meeting. The training was usually held at a big hotel and included demonstrations for how to recruit, how to prospect, and how to sell. At the same time, I wasn't getting very many demonstrations, and I told John how much time I had to study—that I didn't have time to work.

"I'd like you to give a talk about scheduling time for our weekly sales meeting," he said.

"I don't know anything about that," I said.

"Well, just figure it out and come up with something to tell them."

At our next meeting, in front of a bunch of college guys and after a lot of thought, I got up, went to the chalkboard, and drew out a schedule: "Here are all the times of the day, and here are the days of the week. The first time you need to schedule is your most important thing: your classes."

I glanced at the team. They seemed to still be paying attention, so I continued, "If you did it right, you arranged your classes Monday, Wednesday, and Friday between 8:00 and 12:00. Now, notice that that takes only fifteen to eighteen hours of the week, and you have 168 hours. So let's see—what else have you got? The professor says you should put in two hours of preparation for every hour of recitation. None of you go to bed before midnight, so we'll put that at night, from 9:00 to 12:00."

I kept drawing on the chalkboard until I'd finished, then turned around and said. "I want you to look at how much time you've got left over for two or three demonstrations a week. And if you really want to work, you can work on Saturday because the gals are all home on Saturday." And at the same time, the discovery shocked me—I still had plenty of time for eating, for studying, for playing, and for work. John didn't tell me how to do it; he gave me the job so I'd learn from experience, like how Dad had taught us life lessons.

We ended up using that scheduling model through the cookware business, the bra business, and the lingerie business to help our team incorporate balance. We developed it into the form below called "Plan of Progress" that everybody received in their kits.

Plan of Progress
for
Name _____ Date _____

	Sunday	Monday	Tuesday	Wednesday	Thursday	Friday	Saturday
7:00 - 8:00							
8:00 - 9:00							
9:00 - 10:00							
10:00 - 11:00							
11:00 - 12:00							
12:00 - 1:00							
1:00 - 2:00							
2:00 - 3:00							
3:00 - 4:00							
4:00 - 5:00							
5:00 - 6:00							
6:00 - 7:00							
7:00 - 8:00							
8:00 - 9:00							
9:00 - 10:00							
10:00 - 11:00							
11:00 - 12:00							

Colesce Couture International, Inc. • 9004 Ambassador Row • Dallas, TX 75247-4524 • #1801 • Copyright 1999 • Printed in USA • 8/1999

An Example Plan of Progress

In addition to techniques like the Plan of Progress, we motivated our team with expense-paid trips to nearby resorts similar to the trip I won to the Shangri La dude ranch. In keeping the college-age spirit, the team leaders rallied guys and teams to challenge each other to ridiculous things, such as the loser had to swallow a goldfish or eat a dozen raw eggs. Their imagination was unlimited. I never did have to eat the raw eggs, but I did swallow a live goldfish.

Lesson: Facts Tell, Stories Sell

Later that same summer, John and I took thirty-three guys on the road. All of us driving our own cars, we caravanned from Beaumont, Texas, to Memphis, Tennessee. To save money, we slept in our cars when we stopped at night. Luckily we were on highways, not freeways, and were able to find vacant fields to sleep in. We circled the cars, ate the food we'd brought along, and tried to sleep without worrying whether a farmer would come run us off his land.

In Memphis, we found an area of town with two big old mansions whose owners were renting out rooms, so we piled all the guys into those two houses and went to work. I rediscovered my rhythm with selling, practiced the steps, and soon found the process could be as easy as baking a cake. In contrast to Dad's experience with WearEver, where he'd go to someone's house and cook a roast with all the vegetables without water, during our demonstration we pointed out the features and showed our prospects how well the cookware conducted heat. After explaining how it cooked without water because it worked like a miniature oven, I'd say, "Just to show you what I mean, let me bake a cake for you."

Their eyes would drift to the side, recalling all the ingredients and time it took to bake a cake, and they'd say, "Oh, now, you don't have to do that." "Let me show you how easy it is."

So I'd take the Betty Crocker cake mix, stir it up with water in a bowl, and pour it into a little one-quart saucepan before covering it and placing it on top of the stove.

"Well, let's go back in, and I'll show you the rest of the product."

While showing all the pieces, I'd explain each one and how they'd help cook more healthfully without water while saving money, highlighting all the key features. This healthier way to cook taught me a lot about nutrition, which helped later to understand the value of Mannatech products. Toward the end of the demonstration, we'd start smelling the cake and go back into the kitchen. Taking off the lid, it would just be perfect. I'd turn the pan over on a plate and it would fall out perfectly. Then I'd take a Hershey bar and break it off on top of the cake, smear the chocolate out, and slice it—and we'd have a piece of cake. It was an easy, effective, and tasty way to demonstrate how the cookware worked.

Strategy: Be Smart with Money

After that summer in Memphis, John decided Beaumont was too small a town for him, so when he got the opportunity to open the Oklahoma market, he moved his new wife to Oklahoma City.

"Where do you want to go to school?" he asked.

"I was planning on going to Abilene Christian College," I said.

He had gone there, and it was where I wanted to learn how to be a teacher and a preacher.

"I'd like for you to go to Midwestern University in Wichita Falls. It's a good school, not too far from where I'll be, and you can open the town up."

My priority was following Dad's order to get a degree, so I went to Midwestern University and concentrated on my studies. But frankly, I wasn't good at opening a town on my own—I just couldn't seem to do it by myself. Even though it was depressing, I reasoned even Jesus had sent his disciples out two by two! John suggested coming to Oklahoma City, and I started going to school down the road, at Central State College. In between classes, I worked to recruit, build a team, and get ready for the summer selling season.

After that summer, Tom Beam, a friend from church, asked me if I would manage a satellite store where he needed a night manager to work from 1:00 to 9:00 p.m. This worked well with school, and it was a slow time for the college program. He was constantly on the radio—a very successful man, well known for his seat covers. He'd also become enamored with seat belts, which car dealers didn't even sell at the time. So I also looked after a small seat belt manufacturing business while selling and installing seat covers and seat belts.

Looking back, I realized we pioneered the manufacture, sales, and installation of seat belts in Oklahoma. Tom forecasted that one day, seat belts would be so important that the manufacturer would actually put them in every car. Imagine!

Tom told me, "First you gotta come in and learn the business from the ground up," so I learned how to stretch the seat covers by taking a little U-shaped metal ring, like a hog ring, and putting it in a pair of pliers to attach the cover to the bottom ring around the seat. We bought the rings in five-gallon buckets, and they were everywhere. When we'd grab handfuls and put them in our aprons, some would always fall out on the floor.

One day when Tom was showing me around, he stopped to pick up every ring and put it in the barrel. Then I noticed he did this every time he saw one on the floor. He saw me noticing and said, "Stan, you're probably wondering why I do this."

"Yeah," I said. "It seems like a waste of your time."

"Well," he said, "I make about 5 percent at the end of the year. When I add up all my expenses and sales, do the deductions, I end up making about 5 percent. So that means out of every dollar sold, I get to keep a nickel. If I pick up one of these that cost a nickel, it's like making a dollar's worth of sales."

In that moment, he taught me one of my first lessons in how to run a profitable business: *cutting expenses is like increasing sales or as Franklin said, "a penny saved is two pennies clear."* This impacted me so strongly that I have been called a "penny pincher," but that is okay as long as it is about my comments on a company's financial condition on how and where to save.

Lesson: Love Can Change Your Life

In fall 1957, on the brink of my twenties, my life changed in a moment. While attending Central State College, I attended different churches. But on one particular Sunday, I was at my home church sitting with a group of teenagers when I saw a gal come in with her friends. She was prettier than anyone I'd ever seen, and I punched Jimmy Ridgeway, the guy next to me, and said, "Look at that gal—I'm going to marry her."

Someone asked me how I knew that. In thinking about it since, I realized one of my goals in life was to find the girl of my dreams and have a family. When I saw Judy, it was like overlaying a picture of my dream girl and finding her a perfect match.

So I introduced myself to this gal, Judy, and started to get to know her over coffee at church gatherings. She didn't know it at the time, but I was courting her even though she was already engaged. When she came back from Christmas break, she'd decided he wasn't the one, and after the first of January, I met her at the church, and we began to talk more seriously. She gave the gentleman the ring back, and six months later, Judy and I married and started a new chapter of life, embarking on the greatest journey of love and family together.

I looked all over every store
To find a card to tell a new
Of how my love grows more and more
But no one seemed to know of you
I guess its hard to put in rhyme
a love with so much beauty
But in the years that pass with time
I will take it as my duty..
Not just this one day of every year
Will I take time to tell a few
Of the joy of every smile and tear
But all through life I'll love you,

Poem to Judy, Valentine's Day 1958

Marriage is an ancient ritual practiced by all civilizations. It's the result of man's need for love and companionship. An ancient Korean proverb says, "There is no winter without snow. There is no spring without sunshine, and there is no happiness without companionship."

Through her love and companionship, Judy strengthened my why and showed me how one person could make all the right difference in the world. As Victor Frankl eloquently said, "[a] man who becomes conscious of the responsibility he bears toward a human being who affectionately waits for him, or to an unfinished work, will never be able to throw away his life. He knows the 'why' for his existence and will be able to bear almost any 'how.'"

Stan and Judy on their wedding day

The Prophet, by Kahil Gibran

"Love has no other desire but to fulfill itself. But if you love and must needs have desires, let these be your desires: to melt and be like a running brook that sings its melody to the night. To know the pain of too much tenderness. To be wounded by your own understanding of love; and to bleed willingly and joyfully. To wake at dawn with a winged heart and give thanks for another day of loving; to rest at noon and meditate love's ecstasy; to return home at eventide with gratitude; and then to sleep with a prayer for the beloved in your heart and a song of praise upon your lips."

Lesson: More Luck with the Law of Averages

In spring 1959, when I was finishing my senior year, John asked me to join a new company he and a college friend had started and launch a special division. I'd intended to go to graduate school at Oklahoma University, but to qualify for in-state tuition, I'd have to lay out a year. So I thought, *Well, I'll just sell pots and pans the rest of this year and enroll in graduate school next year.* Fortunately, that never happened.

By this time, the cookware business had evolved. Instead of showing a complete set of cookware, you'd show one piece of cookware and concentrate on selling China and crystal. John told me that his groups weren't as strong as the ones we built with a complete set of cookware, so I said, "Well, if you'll help me get these guys set up with a complete set of cookware when they join, then I'll do it." We worked out a plan where a guy could come in and with his first sale of cookware, he gave up the commission and got to keep the complete set he used to demonstrate. Our recruiting criteria were also simple: we joked that "if you could see lightning, hear thunder, and talk," you qualified to be a salesman. We learned to never judge whether a person can be good at selling. Otherwise, I never would have made it.

We would send out postcards to the freshman and sophomore men in the school directory that asked *How would you like to earn $50 to $150 a week? If you're interested in working part-time, call this number.* When prospects called, we'd ask their name and then, instead of asking them yes-or-no questions, we'd give them two options: "I have an opening at five o'clock or seven o'clock—which would you like?"

"What's this all about?" they'd ask.

"Come to the interview and I'll explain. So, do you want five, or would seven be better?" And then they'd take the time.

That was a big lesson: Do not ask yes-or-no questions. Give either/or options when selling.

After building a group of ten or fifteen guys, I left my bride, who was pregnant with our first child, to go on the road. Luckily, she was as patient and understanding as she was beautiful.

One of my best memories about recruiting back then was from the next spring in Tempe, Arizona, where I ended up with fifty guys in a classroom at the college for our presentation. We'd built the interview around the fun aspects of the job—talking to girls and making money. At the closing, I said to the crowd, "If you think you'd like try this, you're not afraid of girls, and you'd like to earn $50 or $150 a week, stay and I'll tell you more about this opportunity. If not, you can leave now." The entire room left. Not a single person stayed. It was like being out quail hunting and flushing a covey of quail, watching them rise in unison just out of reach. Talk about crushed! At the time, I was only about twenty years old and still vulnerable. Devastated, I was ready to quit and go home. Instead, I thought, *Nope—Babe Ruth struck out more times than anyone. But he also hit more home runs than anyone.* In his book, *How I Raised Myself from Failure to Success in Selling,* Frank Bettger tells us Babe Ruth's secret was that he was not afraid to fail. He kept on swinging. *I need to keep trying; there's bound to be somebody here.* I had another interview set for an hour later, and I decided to wait and see what happened.

Do not ask yes-or-no questions. Give either/or options when selling.

When the time came, a hundred people filled the room. When I got to that critical moment when I'd find out whether they'd stay, I kept waiting for them to rise like a covey of quail and flock out of the room. To my astonishment, most sat in their chairs—only a couple guys left. Even with the room full, I didn't get them all—more like thirty. We ended up with a great group out of Tempe that summer.

Selling always worked that way for me: I'd have some dark spots, and all of a sudden, I'd have great times as well. I learned that the law of averages works. We memorized a series of numbers and reminded ourselves of it all the time: 20–12–8–5–4–2. If I talked to twenty people, twelve of them would stop and hear the story. Of those who stopped to listen, eight would actually be interested, and five of them would make appointments. After four actually kept the appointment, I'd sell to two, or 10 percent of the original twenty. When following that principle, the process worked. Most of the time, the law of averages could even be beat. But if we tried to get by with fewer contacts, the numbers didn't work; it took at least twenty contacts for the law of averages to kick in.

Halfway through that summer, we could not stand the separation, so I brought Judy on the road with me, even though she was six months along. Traveling around Texas, we continued building and working with the group. We had a lot of fun and grew even closer as we traveled the small towns of West Texas, staying in cheap motels, enjoying the camaraderie of the group and the excitement of how well our products were accepted.

While traveling West Texas that summer, I ran into Joe Ware, my college roommate. He had worked for us a couple of summers before graduating with a degree in Geology. He was currently working for a big oil company, traveling the oil fields of West Texas. I never thought to ask if he wanted to change careers to build a cookware business, so he asked me. Throughout my sixty years in direct selling, I have been amazed at how many people with college degrees and professional careers turn to direct selling. Several of these people really stood out in the early days when their production made a difference in the ultimate success of the business. Most went on to create their own businesses. Joe Ware went on to create his own pharmaceutical company and Houston Goodspeed, his own insurance business, whom we still work with today. Merwyn Majors owned the first portable building company and many more I do not have all the details to mention.

As the decade drew to a close, I spent a lot of time helping John with the new business. I was beginning to realize that with a baby on the way, I needed to get serious about building a business. I would soon discover that I'd be facing many challenges to overcome, with lessons on the way.

CHAPTER 2

THE VALUE OF EDUCATION

"Whatever the mind can conceive and believe, it can achieve."
Napoleon Hill

Dad stressed the importance of an education because it was his dream and represented a way out of the poorhouse for us. I believe that experience is the best school, but I also realize deep knowledge and skills can be acquired through literature, by learning from the words, thoughts, and ideas of great minds. As Shakespeare had a character observe in Henry VI, "[I] gnorance is the curse of God, and knowledge the wings wherewith we fly to heaven." Books can help you form a life of your own design.

By the start of the 1960s, in addition to the Bible, five books were playing a pivotal role in my life and helping shape my outlook: *Think and Grow Rich* by Napoleon Hill; *Psycho-Cybernetics* by Dr. Maxwell Maltz; *Explorations in Awareness* by J. Samuel Bois; *The Human Side of Enterprise* by Douglas McGregor, and *Atlas Shrugged* by Ayn Rand. The combination of these books and my decision to get serious about building a business supported me in doing just that. Since my early experience with the bumblebee, I had recognized that our minds, and therefore our bodies, are susceptible to outside influence, it becomes a question of what we choose to feed the mind. *Psycho-Cybernetics* and *Think and Grow Rich* expanded on and helped me learn the importance of positive thinking, writing down goals, visualizing, and creating my own "kitchen cabinet"—a brain trust I could rely on.

23

Explorations in Awareness taught me that what people hear us say may not be what we meant. Words like *never, always, completely, everyone, forever* tend to cut off thought and discussion. A group of friends and I used this book to guide our thinking as we built a new Church of Christ congregation to help us transition from an extremely legalistic religious background to a more accepting, loving approach to Christianity. McGregor's *The Human Side of Enterprise* shared his observation that most managers thought of employees as being in two classes, which he defined as *x* and *y*. The *y* individuals were motivated, driven employees; they were rare. Most employees were thought of as *x*—lazy and unambitious, needing authoritative management to get them to be productive. He showed how most people are *y* if given a chance. *Y* employees will exercise self-control and are self-directed when properly motivated. I first heard of *participative management* in his book, which drew on everyone's ideas to develop an answer to problems and manage a business. The question became not what kind of employee is this person, but what kind of manager am I. It was the opposite of the *x* and *y* theory.

Psycho-Cybernetics and *Think and Grow Rich* expanded on and helped me learn the importance of positive thinking, writing down goals, visualizing, and creating my own "kitchen cabinet" –a brain trust I could rely on.

My first experience with this was when we decided to evaluate the effectiveness of our training manual in the cookware business. It was a word-for-word guide that had been used without question for years. Our research found that successful salespeople did not use it word-for-word as recommended. So we did the once unthinkable and ended up rewriting it, based on input from the best salespeople, which resulted in a substantial increase in closing averages.

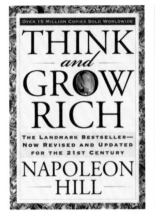

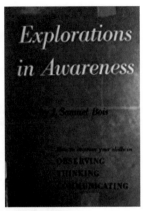
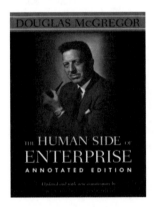

Recommended Reads

Strategy: Follow Fear, Say Yes to Opportunity, and Take Action

To achieve our dreams, we must set goals, believe, *and imagine it will be so.* I've also learned that we must not be misguided by fear—we must look for opportunity and say *yes* to it as well as taking action.

By the end of 1962, the new business that my brother and Tom Fullerton had formed hadn't quite gained traction, and my group was the only division left. We reorganized it under the name Colony House, with John, Tom, and I as partners. By this time, Judy and I had two children, Julie and Stan II, and several families needed to be supported by this business, which just wasn't creating enough revenue to support all of them.

Regal Ware, a company known for manufacturing high-quality stainless-steel cookware, asked us to let them build a set of private-label cookware so that we could set up and go anywhere in the world. John and I discussed the opportunity and loved the idea of having our own design, our own name, and an exciting new opportunity, but the size of the investment required to have our own label cost too much for us at the time.

"We appreciate the offer, but that's too much for us right now," I said.

"How about we lend the money to you? Y'all can pay us back by adding ten dollars a set to your purchases until it's paid off."

So we developed the cookware brand, and my group started selling the Colonial cookware set, paying off the debt very quickly. Working with Regal Ware broadened our perspective, connections, and reach. I've always been thankful for the Reigle family's belief in us, which led them to extend us that much credit.

We began to look for investors to fund the business and help it grow and found a company called Diversa, a small venture capital firm in Dallas led by Gerald Mann, who agreed to invest in exchange for an option on 80 percent of the business. Giving up control was tough to take, but it seemed like the only option. We began to grow and develop the business. We were fortunate, and soon after the transaction, our contact at Diversa called me in for a meeting and delivered some shocking news: "I know you are the youngest partner, but we want you to be the one who runs this whole business. I'm only going to deal with you, and you have to deal with your partners."

Stunned, I sat down with my brother, his partner Tom, and the other four guys who were working for us and said, "Guys, they've asked me to be the chairman, be their only contact, and run the company. I just don't know if I can do it or not. I'm not prepared to run this whole thing."

After the meeting, John called me aside and said, "Let me tell you something, little brother: Don't ever admit your fears in front of people who work for you—you can do this. You're smart enough to do it. I want you to do it. I like you being the chairman; you just go ahead and run it. Run the whole thing like you've been running your division."

With John's voice in my ear, I took on the responsibility. This experience, along with Judy's unwavering faith in my abilities, formed a philosophy I've held to ever since about an energetic belief transference: when someone believes in another person, it releases a power within the other person. Think about the barmaid and Don Quixote in the musical, "The Man Of La Mancha," whose belief transformed her from a barmaid into the beautiful Princess Dulcinea.

Although the working partnership with Diversa was great, they made it clear they were after a faster-growing business than we were going to be. Since we weren't going to grow quickly enough, I needed to find somebody to take over their position. After brainstorming some different people and places to get money, one of the companies that stood out was in Dallas, run by a man named Harry Lemons: Saladmaster, or SMC Industries, its public company name, a company that spawned many successful people, such as Zig Ziglar who became one of the most successful speakers, authors, and personal development coaches of all time. It was nice to know him before—and after—he became famous. I got to know much of Zig's work quite by accident.

To achieve our dreams, we must set goals, believe, *and imagine it will be so.*

Years later, I was on an airplane and all of a sudden, Zig sat down beside me, and we started chatting. After talking about some of his books, I mentioned our lingerie and showed him a catalog. With that token twinkle in his eye, he said, "Okay, I'll send you a collection of books if you'll send me a collection of your lingerie for my wife, 'the little red head,'" that he often referred to. So, partnerships can take on many symbiotic forms, serving as an exchange of ideas, a collaboration, or even an exchange of goods or materials.

Harry Lemons just happened to be from Antlers, Oklahoma, the same town as my wife, Judy. So, when I finally got him on the phone to tell him what I wanted to do, I said, "By the way, I'm Butch Holton's son-in-law, and I think you know of him. He's a good friend of your executive VP, Bill Amend. You might ask him about that family."

I think that helped, because a day or two later, he expressed interest in my plan and invited John and me over to his house to meet with him and his team. They agreed to take over Diversa's position if John and I could obtain all the outstanding stock that we had handed out to our distributors and employees. All of them accepted the fair offer we proposed, and with that accomplished, SMC exercised their option and made us an 80 percent–owned subsidiary. Saladmaster was a public company, and to my surprise, it kept us as officers of our company, Colony House. Our partner, Tom Fullerton, became vice president of Saladmaster's sales promotion department. John was president of Colony House, and I was chairman. The business began to grow and develop from that point, concentrating on the college student and single, working girl program. We also added a new division, setting up franchise dealers to sell our new Colonial Brand of cookware, headed up by one of our most successful college students Novice Nicholson.

So, partnerships can take on many symbiotic forms, serving as an exchange of ideas, a collaboration, or even an exchange of goods or materials.

In a flash of clarity, I realized that our 20 percent of Colony House wouldn't be worth anything unless we could convert it to SMC Industries stock at a price based on Colony House's increasing growth. I asked for something I didn't think they'd agree to but that I did think was fair to both because it would be accretive to the earning per share: taking our 20 percent interest in Colony House after-tax earnings and dividing it by the SMC earnings per share, yielding the number of shares due to the Fredricks. And that was, in fact, the number of shares we got for Colony House, which made us a substantial shareholder of SMC, a move that proved very helpful later on.

Lesson: Be Open to Diversifying

The business and my family continued to grow. Judy and I had welcomed our third child, Jamie, and by 1966, we'd welcomed our fourth child, Ashly, when Regal Ware put us in contact with a guy from Japan who wanted us to sell our product to him wholesale. That moment proved that this growth phase of the business was a successful strategy. We ran ads in *Salesman's Opportunity* magazine, pitching this set of cookware, which proved to be a very successful way of getting new franchise dealers. At one point, we were the largest US exporter of stainless-steel cookware to Japan.

Colonial House Matched Cookware Set

Philosophy: An Inclusive New Church

Growing up, Mom and Dad were very strong Christians. Their belief laid a foundation for my faith and provided a basis for many fundamentals in my life. From how they served others to how Dad helped start a congregation, they not only lived their beliefs, they practiced them.

So it came naturally in 1964, as a group of us became concerned about the legalistic language of the Church of Christ, that I decided to join a group that wanted to start a new congregation that would act differently and think differently. We called it the Central Church of Christ. It was a major step for us because we were very well known within Church of Christ circles. Several of us, all young men, met regularly to study, pray, and plan for the future of the church. Two very influential of those men were Tom Fullerton, our former partner, and Dr. Ken Rogers, son-in-law of the head of the Bible department at Abilene Christian University. With the oversight of one of the elders, Royce Chism, we worked hard to spread the teachings and the word about this new church. For twelve years, I was heavily involved as a teacher, a deacon, and head of the worship committee.

The congregation was soon branded a "liberal church." In those days, being called liberal in the Church of Christ would restrict growth, but despite efforts to ostracize us, we became influential in the Church of Christ world and grew from 14 members to 750. We adopted many practices that, while not new to religion, were new to the Church of Christ: forming a choir, engaging in responsive readings, women reading scripture during the service, singing about the forgiving nature of grace during communion, and accepting all believers. Many members told me they had dropped out of the Church of Christ because they did not feel accepted—but at Central, they felt they belonged. Fifty years later, the survivors of that group are still friends who get together regularly.

Philosophy: Believe in Your Dreams

Since we were young boys, John and I had dreamed of living the bucolic life and owning a thousand-acre ranch for our families. In 1968, a friend of ours from church, Royce Chism, drove us to look at some land just outside of Saint Jo, Texas, where his family had homesteaded in the 1800s. I had no intention of buying any land at that time until the road dropped seven hundred feet off of the prairie, and I saw the magnificent, sprawling hills across the valley. The acreage featured deep, eroded canyons where water had once rushed to the nearby Red River, and where there weren't canyons, there were briars, brambles, and mesquite thickets. I tried to capture that feeling in the poem below:

The Day Spring Came to the Valley

The valley is hidden beyond the plain,
Surprising the eye with its suddenness
And the mind with its majesty
So that each time is like the first time
When I see its hills and trees
The hollows, the meadows, and the leaves.
The last hint of winter is in
The scent of cedar,
The coolness of the earth,

Clumps of dry buffalo grass,
And the sounds of silence.
Then suddenly my senses are shattered
By the coming of spring:
I see the hills in patterned hues of green
Rising toward the bluish haze of the horizon.
I smell the fragrance of a flower
Plucked from the clutches of a bull nettle.
I hear the call of a quail
Signaling its need for another.
I feel the warmth of the
sun on my body.
And I know the joy of spring
As I kneel beside a newborn calf
That waits, trembling for my touch.
It was like that the day
spring came to the valley.

Spring in the valley

We asked Royce to wait a couple of years until we would be able to buy, but he told us that if we couldn't buy it, then he'd have to go ahead and put it on the market.

It was 1968, and we were putting all our money and efforts into Colony House. We had no money to buy land, no matter how much we wanted it, even if it was only $125 an acre. But Royce told us that if we really wanted to start buying land, then he would carry the note. This would be the beginning of the journey to realizing our dream of owning a thousand-acre ranch. We purchased Royce's eighty-eight acres of briars and gullies off a dirt road in northwest Cook County and added to it bit by bit as neighboring properties became available. In the beginning, the property was more a farm than a ranch per se, but it eventually grew to 1,010 acres that would play a pivotal role in our lives and businesses. Not only would our children have the opportunity to work and play on the land, but the acreage would evolve into a home for several business ventures in the years to come.

Not long after we bought those eighty-eight acres, we found that raising cattle was tough: there wasn't enough grass, the cows got lost in the thickets, and the calves got stranded in the canyons. Even $125 an acre began to look expensive. So I asked a neighboring farmer what he thought the land was worth. He thought a minute, spat some tobacco juice, and said, "Twenty-five dollars an acre, just like always. 'Course it will bring more, but it's only worth twenty-five."

In the years to come, we came to understand his wisdom. People are now paying as much as six to ten thousand dollars an acre for the same land.

Strategy: Know When to Pivot and View Failures as Feedback

John and I continued to sell and run the cookware business for four years, but as the decade drew to a close, installment interest rates increased from 5 or 6 percent to 21 percent, which made it very expensive for women to purchase five hundred dollars' worth of anything on credit, and getting finance companies to buy the paper was getting very difficult. SMC had only enough capital to finance about 30 percent of sales. Later on, things got so bad that we asked the Direct Selling Association (DSA) whether they could help. We reasoned that other high-ticket direct-sales companies must have the same issue, so if we could use our collective influence, we might persuade some of the large finance companies to buy our paper. DSA future president Neil Offen arranged for us to meet with the board of directors of Beneficial Finance Co., then the largest commercial loan company in the United States. They sent Alan Luce, one of their young lawyers, with me to meet with Beneficial. Three great things happened on that trip:

First, we convinced them to open their offices all over the United States to buy direct-selling companies' customer contracts.

Second, I watched a future star of the industry at work. After my presentation, Alan, like a seasoned trial lawyer, told a story perfectly calculated to convince them of how important it would be to the industry for them to open up their offices to buy our contracts: "This reminds me of the argument between the chicken and the hog: who was the most important to creating a great breakfast of ham and eggs? The chicken declared she was, because everyone knows how great eggs are. They can be scrambled, boiled, or fried and still taste delicious. The hog replied, 'While all that's true, you have to remember that while you make a great *contribution,* for us hogs, it's a *total sacrifice.*'" The board members all laughed and ultimately recommended that their offices begin buying our paper.

Third, and most important, I was blessed with a friend, partner, and colleague. Alan Luce went on to become general counsel for Tupperware Brands and the CEO of several great names in direct selling, a consultant to the industry named to the Direct Selling Education Foundation's Circle of Honor in 2002 and to the Direct Selling Hall of Fame in 2005. Alan was on a Zoom call, consulting with us at Wine Shop At Home just a few weeks before he passed. His legacy will live on as Brett Duncan, the co-founder, took over Strategic Choice Partners, and will continue to consult and inspire the industry.

John and I began exploring ideas for products that we could sell for cash and ones that women could sell. After all, more women were entering the workforce and needing at least a part-time income.

We tried several different items before landing on one that worked, but we stayed persistent and looked at each "failure" as feedback. We'd learned to never, ever give up, because it's only a true failure if you stop trying. You haven't failed until you quit trying.

At the time, wigs were quite popular, so we sold wigs, but they could not build a big business. Then one day, after reading a magazine article on the emerging "peacock generation," which described how men were beginning to use skin care products and colognes, I thought *Hey, that would make a* great *direct-sales item.*

I asked John, "What if we created a line of colognes for men—one that would be soft and sensual, romantic for the evening, and another more robust, masculine one for the day?"

"That's a great idea," he said. "What are we going to call it?"

"How about Alpha and Omega? Alpha for the beginning of the day and Omega for the end."

We researched, contacted chemists, and started to develop our lines. After selecting the fragrances, we recruited women to go into offices to sell and show them to the men in person. Their opening line when the receptionist asked what a saleswoman wanted with the boss? "Just tell him it's something personal." They almost always got in to see the boss. In the beginning, sales were astounding. Several women performed extremely well, nearly convincing us that we'd landed on our ideal product. We soon found that the problem—or, rather, the lesson—was in direct selling, the business grows when your customers can become your salespeople. In our case, the women sold to men, but the men didn't go on to sell to other men. The business grew in spurts, and when it didn't gain more traction, we shelved the idea.

Around this time, Judy began wearing a beautiful bra made by Penny Rich, who had become a phenomenon and was known for selling a special custom-fitted design. Using a network marketing model similar to Amway's, Penny had expanded all over the country. When she had a falling out with a manufacturer in Puerto Rico, she lined up another one in Frederick, Oklahoma—no relation. I called up the guy who was manufacturing the bra for her, an interesting man named N. O. Brantley, and set up a time to tour the factory. Brantley had invented the two-way stretch material that made the girdle and bra industry possible. Before then, bras stretched only one way and weren't as comfortable.

You haven't failed until you quit trying.

Brantley also loved to fly. At one time he'd had a contract to deliver the US mail by plane, and that had inspired him to design a personal helicopter, thinking it the transportation method of the future. His partner told him he should concentrate on one business or the other, so he sold the elastic company interest to his partners but came out ahead through royalties on his patents from factories in seven countries. Brantley eventually sold the helicopter business to Learjet and started making foundation garments.

When I arrived in Oklahoma, Brantley started showing me the different equipment and asked, "So you're interested in a distributorship and going to work for me?"

"No, I don't want to buy the bra. I want to buy the factory."

He chuckled, but we kept talking about the idea. "Well, what's your vision?"

"I'd like for you to stay on to do the engineering and to design the products. I want to own the factory to be able to develop private labels and sell the bras to other companies."

He warmed up to the idea, all in one sitting. A few days later, he called and said, "I found a way that will help you pay for it, but you're going to have to get my ex-wife to agree. I owe her a hundred thousand dollars on a note as part of our divorce settlement. If you can get her to let you take over the loan, I'll do it. My new wife and I would rather not have to deal with her."

We soon found that the problem—or, rather, the lesson—was in direct selling, the business grows when your customers can become your salespeople.

I certainly didn't use those words when I called his ex-wife; instead, I spent some time on the phone with her, listening to her grievances and hearing her side of the story. Whatever I said must have struck a chord with her because I convinced her that I was dependable and that I would personally ensure that she received all her money. She must have taken a liking to me—or else she was keen on the idea of not having to put up with Brantley any more—because she agreed to let me take over the note payment. And so Cameo, our custom-fit bras and lingerie company, was born.

It is important to partner with the people in life who can step into the mentor role, and Brantley would become an important mentor and partner of mine. He taught me how to make bras and shared the design elements that they used in designing his helicopter: providing suspension, producing thrust, and defying gravity—information that would evolve into part of the sales pitch for Cameo. Following is a copy of the drawing used to apply for the patent for this very unique bra.

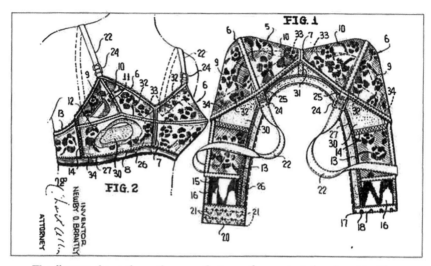

The diagram above shows the many features of our patented custom-fitted bra. This is why we are able to eliminate so many of the problems that cause a regular bra to not fit properly. The theory behind the bra is that it holds the bust within a triangle and supports the breast on a suspension-type camberband. The bras shown here were engineered by N.O. Brantly, an aeronautical engineer and the brilliant creator of the first machine to make two-way stretch fabrics.

Brantley Patent Illustration

Brantley explains engineering of the bra to new owners.

As fate or our Creator's divine sense of humor would have it, I made the deal and signed the papers on May 5, 1970, and on July 4, women began throwing their bras into a burning barrel at Berkeley in California. The newspaper headlines about women burning their bras convinced our public, so we were teased that the Fredrick family would be going bust—the bra had hit its peak. Our response was calm: "It's like the old story about the pessimist and the optimist who were given an African territory to sell shoes: The pessimist wrote back to the home office and said, 'I'm coming home. This territory is lousy. No one wears shoes.' The optimist wrote, 'This territory is great. Everyone is a prospect. They don't have any shoes.'"

We struggled in the beginning, but as is always the case in direct selling, it only takes one person to see and seize an opportunity. If people go without bras, eventually gravity will guarantee that they need one. As it turned out, we'd have the last laugh because our bra business would expand rapidly in the years to come.

★★★

Lesson: Teach Children the Value of Money and Instill a Work Ethic in Them

Son Stan II's First Experience in Direct Sales

As a ten-year-old, I went to the bike store and found the exact bike I wanted–a coffee-colored Vista Cruiser ten-speed that cost $99.95. I told Dad about the bike and how much I wanted it.

At Christmas, I didn't get the bicycle. In February, my birthday came and went without receiving a bicycle. Summertime was approaching, and I couldn't get over how much faster my friends were on their ten-speeds than I was on my single-speed. I must've pestered Dad enough that one day he came home from work carrying a big brown box. "Dad, what's in the box?" I asked.

"This is your ten-speed, son."

Perking up, I started thinking I must have to put it together, but when he set the box down, I opened it up to find it was full of candles.

"What are these?"

"Those are one for three dollars, two for five dollars."

Over the next couple of days, he taught me how to make a presentation. Pretty soon, I put on my army green backpack, stuffed full of candles, and walked the neighborhoods to sell them door to door until I'd earned the money to buy that ten-speed.

From that early experience, I learned the power of having a goal; that any goal is achievable, if you have the will, the work ethic, and the right vehicle to make it happen.

Daughter Ashly's Lesson on Personal Responsibility and Managing Money

Growing up, there were so many lessons. We worked from the time that we could work. My earliest memory of being at the office was in elementary school and going off to work in downtown Dallas with my sister, Jamie. We had a great time while learning as little girls how to work early in life. I learned the value of working and the value of personal responsibility. I learned how you are responsible for how you show up. You're responsible for putting in a full day's work and doing your very best at it. You are responsible for managing the money, sending some to savings, and then getting to play with the rest.

Later on, when Jamie and I got to high school, Dad and Mom decided to give us an allowance but not just *give* us an allowance. They tallied up all the money for our expenses for a month. We thought this was cool—we'd be getting *this much* money in a month. But we really had to learn how to manage our money because it bought our clothes, our shoes, and our makeup. If we wanted to get our hair cut, it bought that.

I'll never forget how Dad gave us a cash journal to write down where we spent the money and then made us show it to him before we'd receive our next check for the following month. He taught us how to manage money and learn where our money went and how it was being spent.

> When I graduated and got ready to get married, I worked for myself and had to pay taxes, so knowing how to manage money and how to organize for taxes and savings was very valuable. It was easier to be in that budgeting mind-set.

Ashly is an example of our family motto, *Never Ever Give Up*. She overcame dyslexia and other learning difficulties, thanks in part to Judy's diligence, and evolved to be our best student, teacher, and speaker.

After graduating from Abilene Christian University with a degree in Corporate Fitness, she began a lifelong career of learning so she could help her clients overcome unhealthy habits and disruptive emotions. She has completed several advanced certifications in fitness, emotional resolution, and eating psychology.

These help her teach and motivate clients to live with increased health and vitality, through her company BioBalance, which emphasizes mind, heart, emotional, and physical balance. Her clients include our Legacy companies Mannatech, Wine Shop, and Custom Fit Bra Company, where she is a sought-after speaker and personal coach. Ashly is the author of the book that ends the diet drama, *The End Zone*.

CHAPTER 3

FINDING CHANNELS OF DISTRIBUTION

"What you get by achieving your goals is not as important
as what you become by achieving your goals."
Henry David Thoreau

In addition to imagining and acting on a dream, don't ever give up—and live for your dream. When women began burning their bras, for the first time in my business career, I wished I had a degree in marketing instead of English. With this new bra venture, we needed to know what channel of distribution to use for this unique product that everybody was burning. Had we known about the four Ps of marketing, we would have said that we had a good *product,* the *price* was consistent with competition, and the features were *promotable*—however the *place* to sell it was a big question mark.

At the time, the traditional channel of distribution for a brassiere company was department stores: buyers sat behind big desks and listened to the factory salesmen who sold their company's product. But the demand for what they had was dropping like a rock, so they weren't eager to add more stock-keeping units (SKUs)—in fact, they were converting floor space to use for other items. The cost of the sales force needed to get the bra on those shelves was prohibitive, and the cost of advertising to get the consumer to create a demand was even worse. The retail channel was closed to us.

The other channel gaining in popularity was mail order, but only Fredricks of Hollywood (again, no relation) was doing anything significant at the time, and ours was definitely not his type of product. But another channel was emerging as a dominant force in retailing—direct selling. And that's the channel that saved us.

Fortunately, John and I knew about direct selling, and we knew it was a good way to sell a product with unique features, one requiring demonstration. So, we began selling our unique custom-fit Cameo bra through direct selling, adding a third channel to the way bras were sold. Direct sales allowed our company to combine two of those four Ps into one because the distribution system was also the way the product was promoted.

Another channel was emerging as a dominant force in retailing– direct selling. And that's the channel that saved us.

On September 7, 1970, we met with a woman named Hassie Burke who agreed to be our first salesperson. During the first full year, we did $150,000 in sales. In ten years, we reached $5 million in sales, thanks in part to our adaptability. Initially our bras were sold through personal home fittings, but over the coming years, we were challenged to come up with alternate solutions, to create something more enticing that would bring women together.

One of the women who helped us with that was a woman whom we made a bra for called Kathy Alls. She had become famous doing infomercials for an exercise product called Slim Jim. She liked our group sales approach and agreed to sell her business and join us to promote the Cameo Bra as our vice president of marketing. She began promotion of the product on radio shows, television, and advertisements in *Woman's Day* and *Cosmo*. The ultimate exposure came with a two-page spread in *People* magazine that resulted in over 5,000 inquiries, most of which resulted in customers and consultants. She was very important in changing our image to the company that overcame the bra-burning fad to one that built a better bra and turned a negative into a positive.

Sales Strategy–the Magic of Common Grounds

Find common ground with customers because doing so builds rapport. Be curious and be genuine, asking questions to discover what you have in common with others. Ask yourself what you can understand about them or their family. Common ground is magic for creating partnerships.

As Cameo continued to grow, so did the family and the farm. Judy and I welcomed our second son and fifth child, Landen, and the early 1970s proved to be a transformative time for the farm. Shortly after our purchasing the land, we ventured into the cattle business. The federal government had decided to sponsor a reclamation project: if landowners put up 10 percent, the government would put up 90 percent—which turned the $100,000 we put up into $1,000,000. The government's money shaped out our canyons and helped turn them into ponds and pastureland. I've never liked government programs, but when I look at our place and see us running two hundred head of cattle on land where we once couldn't have raised a goat, I see that the project did indeed contribute to the future economy.

Lesson: Sometimes Family Relationships Are Worth a Personal Sacrifice

Also at the start of the 1970s, Harry Lemons decided to sell his interest in Saladmaster to an investment company out of Houston led by Jeff Dyke and a team of investors. In the initial restructuring, they appointed Bill Amend chairman, but when the business didn't grow for a couple years, they asked him to resign and run the finance company instead.

One day in early 1973, I was surprised when the head of the new owners called and asked me to fly to Houston: "I'll have my car pick you up. I want you to come by the office so we can talk."

I didn't know what he wanted, but as we sat down to talk, he handed me a piece of chalk and pointed to the chalkboard, "I want you to tell me …if you were CEO, how you would run this company?"

At the time, SMC Industries included Saladmaster, Nationwide Acceptance, Colony House, MasterGuard, PM Press, True Distance, Frybrant, and Cameo. I'd never thought about running the company, but I did have some ideas, and I drew out for him on the board what I would do and how I would run the business: cutting costs by consolidating and managing the group as a whole rather than as individual companies. Even though the companies were independent, they'd answer to one person. "All right," he said, "you're our next CEO."

Soon after my transition into CEO, a thunderstorm rolled into town while working in my beautiful new office. My desk was near the window at the edge of the building, and although it was in an older building in the industrial part of town, I wasn't worried and continued to work. All of a sudden, the ceiling collapsed, drenching me, the beautiful furnishings, everything. Before I could move, there was two feet of water in my office for a real-life example of "when it rains, it pours." It would have been natural to see this as a bad omen for my new position. Yet, I saw it as funny how I went from a buttoned-up executive in a suit and tie to looking like a drowned rat, looking for a way to escape while at the same time salvaging as much as I could of files and records.

This actually seemed to galvanize the company as a whole to rally around our need to unify and rebuild. Later, I learned the drain for the roof had stopped up, allowing water to collect over my side of the building. The weight was too much for the old roof, causing it to give way, pouring two feet of water all over me and my office. In the end, it all worked out. I got a new roof, a new office, and the opportunity for a new beginning.

Philosophy: When Life Bucks, Get Back on the Horse and Never Ever Give Up

After that interesting interview, I became CEO of SMC Industries for the next two and half years. During that time, things were still difficult with financing: the economy wasn't doing well, what with the Fed fighting

After ten years as President of one of SMC Industries' subsidiaries, it is a pleasure, as the newly elected President of the parent organization, to address you, the shareholders.

From a single product company selling salad machines, SMC has grown to five product groups covering a diversity of merchandise sold primarily in the home and often on a party plan basis.

Revenues for the fiscal year ended August 31 were the best ever. The total of $15,112,584 was up 16% over the 1973 figure of $13,026,058. As a result of certain inventory write-downs related to slow moving merchandise and to reserves established on contracts receivable totalling $600,000, net earnings declined significantly from 1973 figures. The write-downs included $276,000 for inventory in Masterguard and Frybrant. A total of $233,000 was written off for the excess of cost over net assets and for a related note receivable in connection with True Distance, Inc. Saladmaster set up additional reserves of $86,000 on its contracts receivable in Puerto Rico.

Earnings were $328,312, or 40¢ per share, compared to $760,336, or 91¢ per share last year. At the fiscal year close, SMC had $386,317 in cash or the equivalent; working capital was $3,738,258 or $4.44 a share and the return on equity amounted to 7.1%.

The SMC Board, in late May, initiated several management changes which included my election as President and Chief Executive Officer of SMC Industries. J. W. Amend, who has served the company in various capacities for 24 years, moved from President to Vice-Chairman of the Board. He is continuing as President of Nationwide Acceptance Corporation. F. J. Dyke, Jr. of Houston was elected Chairman of the Board.

In another action, Ray E. Jones, who has been an outstanding field executive in Saladmaster for 16 years, was named President of Masterguard Corporation. This move freed Harold Curtis to devote full attention to his duties as Financial Vice President of SMC Industries, after having spent 9 months in the dual role of President of Masterguard and Financial Vice President of SMC.

The minority shareholders of Colony House exercised their rights to exchange their holdings for SMC stock, and the three companies in the Colony House group became wholly-owned subsidiaries directly responsible to the management of SMC.

Saladmaster had another good year of sales increases in its marketing of quality housewares. Masterguard, which is now concentrating on merchandising fire protection systems, recorded a sharp increase in sales in the past year. Due to the decision to de-emphasize burglar alarms, substantial reserves were established on the company's burglar alarm inventory at year end. P:M Press experienced its most successful year in terms of sales and profits.

As a result of long range planning, we have decided to concentrate our efforts on direct-to-home marketing. The basis of this strategy is three product groups – household products, intimate apparel and security systems. Growth in these areas will be achieved primarily through increased recruiting of dealers and distributors. This is the principal way in which sales, and therefore profits, are increased in a direct sales company.

Current economic conditions provide both opportunities and problems to SMC. Increased unemployment and inflation make it easier to recruit quality sales people. However, tight money restricts outside financing sources for our consumer sales contracts. Management expects easing of the current tight money situation in the months ahead to have a beneficial impact on both sales and earnings.

Sincerely,

President
SMC INDUSTRIES, INC.
November 27, 1974

SMC Shareholders Letter, 1974

inflation and high interest rates, and the company wasn't flourishing because finance companies had quit buying our paper. The team of investors had fallen apart. Those who remained decided to replace Jeff, the chairman, so they called a board meeting in Houston.

On the flight there, the CFO sat by me on the airplane and said, "I hate to tell you this, but the reason we're having this board meeting is because they're replacing you as president and CEO, and they're going to make me the president and CEO. But I think they'll give you a good exit package with at least three months' severance. I hate to do that to you, but it's just business."

At their office, we were all sitting around a waiting room when I looked around at the guys and thought, *I'm not going to sit here and let this happen. Somehow, I'm going to figure this out.* Realistically, I realized that I was about to be fired and that I depended on the income for my livelihood. It certainly could have been dire, but I didn't stop and think about it. It was never fatal to me. I repeated to myself, *If things don't work out, it's not the end.* There's a power in choices. One of the choices we make is how we choose to look at things and how to pick our actions accordingly. Why not choose a way that works out for you? The old story about half-full or half-empty is true. Believe that there is a way and that you can figure it out.

Brantley was the first person I'd ever heard talk about focus, although he called it concentrating. He'd said, "When you have a problem, concentrate on it and shut everything else out. Let them think you're unsociable. If you don't concentrate, you won't figure out the solution."

It was a good lesson that I've tried to follow all my life. So, a matter of moments after discovering I'd be fired, I concentrated on figuring out a strategy. I figured out exactly what I needed to do, which was convince them to sell me those two businesses that they didn't like: the bra factory and Cameo. This meant I would be leaving behind my first direct-selling career, the cookware business. Saladmaster eventually sold to Regal Ware, and it is still a successful brand today under leadership of Jeff Reigle, grandson of my old benefactor.

I knew they didn't like the lingerie business, so I decided to play on that fact. In business, it's important to know your alliances. I had to get rid of the guy they were going to make the CEO because if he was in that spot, he wasn't going to sell me the businesses. I thought I could talk Jeff into selling them to me if he was the CEO, so I immediately figured out how to convince them that the current chairman of the board, Jeff, would make a good CEO—that they *needed* him. I had to overcome their displeasure with him, which had prompted them to get rid of him too. I had to convince them that their need for him outweighed the problem they had with him, that the problem was a personal problem and shouldn't interfere with this business.

"I'm going to go to the restroom," I said.

So I got up and went to the restroom, but on the way back, I went looking for the other board members because I knew they'd be meeting somewhere. When I found them and walked in, they said, "Oh, we're not ready for you yet. It's not time."

"I think it is," I said. "I think you need to hear what I have to say."

"First of all, the guy you're replacing me with is a smart guy, but the sales force doesn't like him and wouldn't want to deal with him. You'd be a lot better having Jeff as CEO because the sales force likes him. As far as I'm concerned, I'm encouraging you to fire me and replace me with Jeff."

"We're not going to fire you. We're going to let you resign. We'll make a big story about how great a job you've done."

Believe that there is a way and that you can figure it out.

"I appreciate that," I said. "That's very generous of you. But there's a clause in my contract that says that if you fire me, the noncompete agreement is null and void. I'll be free to go into the cookware business as your competition. It's entirely possible your franchise dealers would want to buy my less expensive brand of cookware. I've spent the past two and a half years getting to know the franchise dealers really well, and I think quite a few of them might come with me. I'm not going to resign—you're going to have to fire me."

"What do you mean? We don't want you to go into competition with us. That could hurt us. What do you want?"

"I'll tell you what, I own a lot of stock in Saladmaster. I'll trade you my stock for the bra business, Frybrant and Cameo.

"Why in the world would you do that? They're losing money."

"I think that if they weren't connected and I were on my own, they could be successful."

They thought and talked about it for a while and said, "Okay, you've got a deal, except it's going to cost you some cash and money."

"I'm not going to have any cash to give you, but I'll sign a note."

I knew about what I could afford and agreed on a formula, and I knew to never, ever give up. I returned to the group in the waiting room, knowing they'd be in for a big shock when the board met and they heard my proposal, which the board had agreed to. The CFO was furious and said I would lose all my stock and go broke. I told him, "Like you said, it's just business."

In reality, my only concern was my brother's reaction because it would be hard to do what I'd planned without him. When I sat down with him, I said, "This is going to be shocking, but they fired me as CEO. But I worked a deal where we can buy Cameo and Frybrant and go off on our own."

"Oh, no—not me," he said. "I'm making good money here. Everything is going smooth. Why would I take that risk?"

"Yes, you'll have to give up your ownership in Saladmaster and being president of Colony House—that's true. But we can finally be partners and own 100 percent of the business. We can make our dreams come true. You will continue as president of Cameo and Frybrant. We aren't going to have shareholders and a board of directors anymore, and we aren't going to be a public company with all the expenses and regulations. And just look at the great opportunity we have in growing this business—it's already growing, and we're going to keep making money. I'll show you how we can keep paying you the same amount while the business keeps making money."

For the next couple weeks, John thought about the idea, and then he decided to go all in. We knew we needed someone to help us with sales in the business, so I suggested bringing on Novice Nicholson, our key man in the cookware business, who had stayed with us over the years, as executive VP of sales. I became chairman and co-CEO, and John served as president and co-CEO. Our management structure was a little unusual, but it worked for us. Novice managed the sales administration and field force, and John handled marketing, merchandising, and distribution. I took care of accounting, manufacturing, IT, and product design. We started with that team structure and grew the business nationally for the next twenty-five years.

Like T. S. Eliot said, "Only those who will risk going too far can possibly find out how far one can go." These experiences helped craft a philosophy: We must never ever lose our sense of optimism, no matter what we face. Even when we get thrown off, we have to get back on the horse and embrace the possibilities that life holds, more than just the risks, dangers, setbacks, and hardships. Optimism distinguishes those who are on the way up from those who are on the way down.

I try to apply this philosophy to all facets of life. Looking for the opportunities in life later helped me do significant things for Cameo and the industry while I served on the Direct Selling Association's board of directors—another parallel element that played a large role in my life and in my growth and development.

Jamie, third child and second daughter

In the fifth grade, I was on a horse that went crazy and took off for a peach orchard. I fell off, but my foot became caught in the stirrup until a tree root knocked me loose. All bloodied up, I remember thinking, *I'm going to have to get back on that horse. Dad will want me back up on that horse*–because that's what we did. If you're going along and you get knocked down, you're going to get back up, and you're going to keep going.

Either that afternoon or the next day, I got back on her, rode her hard, and brought her back. I don't think that he ever said the words *"You need to get back up,"* but I heard him in my head. On horses and in life, he's always in my ear: *You get back on, you get back up, you dust yourself off, and you keep going.*

Strategy: Move from Wages to Wealth by Building a Team

I was lucky enough to find the "how" for my dreams early in life when I discovered the great industry of direct sales. Over the years, John and I found that we could use direct sales to do just about everything:

- Have our own business;
- Be our own bosses;
- Develop our personal skills;
- Pursue our dreams;
- Share our opportunity; and
- Serve others.

Through direct selling, I experienced the joy of being my own boss, the satisfaction of sharing, and the magic of multiplication. Building a team is a way to move from wages to wealth, and I found early on I could have whatever I wanted if I sold one more set, recruited one more person, built one more downline, started one more business, or bought one more company. It's all a matter of sharing opportunity and building people. Direct selling is one of the few places anyone, regardless of race, color, social status, or education, can move up the ladder. It's been said the rung of a ladder is not to stand on but to hold one foot while you raise the other one higher, and direct selling is exactly like that.

Confucius said, "If you plan prosperity for one year, grow grain. If you plan prosperity for ten years, grow trees. If you plan prosperity for a hundred years, grow people."

Gary McDonald, a top executive at Tupperware and a member of the Direct Selling Hall of Fame, was instrumental in developing my sales management approach, and I recommend it to anyone who is building a team or managing a sales force. Making time to routinely call your team members will pay off exponentially in several ways. He recommended we start by asking them three questions: *What are you going to do? How are you going to do it? How did you do?*

Using this approach, you soon find yourself in a position to understand what they're thinking, understand their goals, help them reach their goals, find out whether they've reached their goals—and then start the process all over.

Strategy: Think Long-Term for Future Success

I had always wanted to join the Direct Selling Association, but Saladmaster was very insular and did not associate with others in the industry. So after we bought the bra business, we joined, and in 1974, I went to my first meeting and met the president and other leaders of the association.

At that meeting, I talked to Bob King, president and CEO of World Book, who was the industry leader and chairman of the board for DSA, and told him I wanted to be more involved. A short time later, he called and said, "We'd like you to become chairman of the Development Committee."

"What does that mean?" I asked.

"Well, we want you to recruit new members. And the challenge you're going to have is most members of the association don't want anybody else in. They want us to stay a little club and not involve the other people in the industry. I'd like you to change that and get them excited about bringing in real quality new members."

I thought that was a tall order for a brand-new guy, but I took it on, learned about the association and the members, and started to contact people for appointments. When they asked me to take a young man named Jerry Taylor with me and train him in how to recruit, I used the same method we used to sell cookware: First find a common ground, then answer the most common objection: "It's expensive." "Yes, I'd agree, but this is the 'best bang for the buck' you will ever get for your business." I'd

Direct selling is one of the few places anyone, regardless of race, color, social status, or education, can move up the ladder.

explain the advantages of being a member—having DSA defend us against government regulations and improve our reputation by getting us into colleges and universities, not to mention the camaraderie, exchanges of ideas, and open conversations around successful business practices—before asking them for their dues check. At the next annual meeting, I was surprised to be honored for having recruited more new members and collected more new dues than anyone in the history of the association.

After several years, I switched my attention and helped support the Direct Selling Education Foundation, whose main focus was shifting the negative stereotypes people had about the industry. In my Introduction to Business course in college, the textbook had devoted only a single paragraph to direct selling—and hadn't recommended pursuing it.

The foundation was formed with the idea of getting universities to introduce the real concept of direct selling—what it meant, how lucrative it was, and how quickly it was growing. I'm happy to say that through incredible leadership at the foundation on the part of Marlene Futterman, the small paragraph eventually transformed into entire chapters in textbooks, largely through the collaborative efforts of the Education Foundation Board and Neil Offen, the president of the DSA.

Neil Offen retired after over forty years as the president of the Direct Selling Association. His tenure was marked by great achievements, such as the passing of a law by Congress that protected the independent status of direct-selling distributors. He also guided us through the difficult downturn in business and in membership during the late 1980s. His leadership and development of the association is the stuff legends are made of. It was truly a pleasure and an honor to work with him all those years.

The foundation was formed with the idea of getting universities to introduce the real concept of direct selling–what it meant, how lucrative it was, and how quickly it was growing.

The Direct Selling Association would help us form connections and provide us with many opportunities in the years to come. I was always amazed at how much the DSA and industry leaders listened to executives from small companies like mine as well as big companies like Avon and Amway. At board meetings, I got to know Rich Devos of Amway, Jim Preston of Avon, Mary Kay Ash of Mary Kay, Mary Crowley of Home Interiors, Alan Kennedy of Nature's Sunshine, Bob King of World Book, Erick Lane of Cutco, and Jerry Heffel of Southwestern Books. I thought it part of my duty to help the industry grow as much as I could because I wanted my children and grandchildren to have the same opportunity we had to have our own business.

Over the next forty years, I stayed very involved within the association and the foundation because I wanted to help secure the future of direct selling. By this time, I'd realized that my family and I were going to be in the industry for a long time, and I wanted to help protect its future. I remain very grateful for the industry because I've experienced what it can do for a life and for a family in seeing how it enabled this poor boy from Waco to achieve his dreams and then some.

As chairman of the Direct Selling Education Foundation, I helped codify and institutionalize a practice of asking our members to voluntarily contribute one-third of the amount of their dues to the Foundation. We reasoned that one-third of the Association's dues would be the amount of money that it took to finance the foundation. For many years, I chaired the development committee for the foundation to contact members to explain and encourage this novel way of funding. We called it "giving your fair share" before the phrase went out of favor.

To take the pressure off of the membership, we recommended a capital campaign. The foundation board asked Doug DeVoss of Amway and me to co-chair the Twenty Million Dollar Capital Campaign. The idea was to have enough capital to create an income stream of a million dollars a year that would finance the foundation's programs. Thanks to Amway's generosity and the membership's response to their matching offer of other donors, we raised over twelve million dollars. About this time, the Board changed leadership and decided to take another approach to funding the foundation.

When my term on the Board ended, I did not offer to stand for re-election. It seemed time for me to leave the leadership to the younger generation, which was now the responsibility of Joe Mariano, president of DSA, and the new leadership team to continue the great work of the foundation. It's important to the industry that we support its programs and the awesome academics I worked with for years, such as Dr. Linda Ferrell, Dr. Greg Marshall, and Dr. Robert Peterson. They have increased the credibility of the industry and continue to advocate strongly for our business model.

Sales Lesson: Mary Crowley's *How You Doing?* Calls and Honoring Leaders

I learned a lot from Mary Crowley of Home Interiors. After we connected through DSA, I asked her how she built her business. She said, "With *how you doing?* calls: I make it a point to call my leaders regularly and ask them how they are doing."

Over the call, you find out the problems you didn't know they had and the challenges they're going through, and then you can start to use that opportunity to help them over their challenges and inspire them to the next level.

We began to call our leaders every week to make sure they knew that we were thinking about them and that we were going to help grow their business. Those calls became an integral part of our business.

Another idea of hers we instituted was what she called a mountain-top experience for her new leaders. It was a high-level training class at her house in the mountains of Colorado. We duplicated this with our Regional Schools at the ranch.

CHAPTER 4

RESPECT RELATIONSHIPS AND PARTNERSHIPS

"A thing of beauty is a joy for ever:
Its loveliness increases; it will never
Pass into nothingness."
John Keats

Lesson: Family Is the Priority–It Is a Thing of Beauty

I have learned to see life itself as a thing of beauty, a dream open to intent. My life creations have included businesses, homes, art, and, most important, relationships. Family was always my number-one priority, a lesson Dad taught me.

At the start of the 1980s, Judy's and my home had been full of life's beauty. Defining values helps in prioritizing the tasks at hand and maintaining a sense of balance. People often neglect one aspect of their life in pursuit of greatness in another, but as the years became busier and the businesses grew, I never questioned or thought of neglecting one for the other. I saw it more as tending to each as you would rows of various

55

plants or herbs in a garden: each has different needs, and you take action accordingly.

Growing up, not only did Dad instill in me that family was the number-one priority, but he also taught us to have deep respect for women. He'd told us, "I remind myself how lucky I am every day," and he demonstrated that by revering my mother, complimenting her, and doting on her. Growing up as I did in a male-dominated family, Dad's respect for Mom throughout their seventy-six-year marriage deeply influenced my personal and professional life.

Later in life, Dad shared marriage advice at a friend's wedding that included a favorite Bible verse, James 1:19: "Everyone should be quick to listen, slow to speak, and slow to anger." Other pieces of wisdom included the following:

- Always listen to the other's viewpoint;
- Find something to compliment the other about daily;
- Always place the other first in your plans;
- Say *I love you*—daily;
- Never go to bed angry with each other;
- Start your day by having breakfast with each other; and
- Let coming together at the end of the day be its greatest accomplishment.

A few years ago, I tried to instill these same values as I officiated my granddaughter Presley's wedding. See ceremony in the appendix.

Landen, second son and fifth child

"Dad taught us how to be good parents and spouses through his love and devotion to Mom. My parent's devotion to each other was best portrayed during their difficult times with their health; first my father with his hip and then my mother with leukemia. Over months, whether at home, in the hospital, or a rehabilitation home, they never left the other's side. We would try and relieve them and give them a break so they could get rest, but they would always resist us and stay huddled close to each other. Oftentimes, we would walk in the hospital room and find them sleeping together, holding each other in the tiny hospital bed. My dad believes in the power of love, commitment, and loyalty.

He has built a family legacy rich with traditions we now pass on to the next generations."

Strategy: Test Different Approaches and Pay Attention to Social Trends

I believe in the power of the direct-selling model and the opportunity it creates for anyone to own and run a business. Cameo, in particular, helped women step into the role of being architects who designed their lives and environments to include more income, fantasy, illusion, and individual expression. I love the Henry James observation, "The mold of a woman's future and the shape of her life and destiny, the sum total of all her accomplished achievements, are in her own hands that holds the invisible brush that paints pictures on the walls of her mind."

Respect for women carried over from the personal into the professional realm, and I credit Cameo's success to women, who were the largest factor in Cameo's success. At the time, more and more women were entering the workforce, and their entrepreneurial spirit shaped us, much as the bras they sold helped shape the women who wore them.

A business and its people must be receptive to change and open to modifications, and the women on our team were always willing to act and adapt. In 1980, the owner of Figuerettes, whom I had met at DSA, asked me to buy his company. Their product line was similar to ours yet included nutrition, jewelry, and sleepwear. The number one consultant then was Kathleen Leinen who still orders bras from us today, thirty years later.

Cameo grew steadily, though not dramatically. Yet, the addition of Figuerettes jumpstarted our growth as we added more products, cosmetics, supplements, jewelry, perfumes, and more bras. In the mid- to late-1980s, pieces of sleepwear and loungewear that we offered as add-ons to bra customers were becoming major sellers. Working women were beginning to ask for sexier lingerie and more exotic sleepwear.

Helen Gurley Brown and *Cosmopolitan* magazine were reflecting a cultural shift by which, although women wanted to show that they could compete in a man's world, they also wanted to still be feminine. *Cosmo* even ran a feature article on "Cleopatra Syndrome," noting that women also wanted to be their own person: they wanted their clothing and their lingerie to reflect who they were or how they were feeling. A lot of women liked to play—imagining that they were Cleopatra, as it were—and were buying lingerie that empowered them to do so.

We carried that article around with us, letting people see it. Having witnessed the success of party-plan companies, such as Mary Kay and Tupperware, we decided to test a pure party-plan lingerie program with a group of sales ladies who were accustomed to selling through home parties. The results were phenomenal. Sales went from zero to a million dollars in a year, with a projected growth rate at the 40 to 50 percent rate.

The hostess-driven party plan method used the same lingerie, but how it was shown was more fun for the salesperson, more profitable for the hostess, and more exciting for the guests, making recruiting and booking parties easier. The party-plan design excited the women into trying the items, with the theory that romancing the item helped romance the self. The consultant mixed and showed about twenty items, but what we were really selling was feelings, fantasies, and a sense of well-being.

Respect for women carried over from the personal into the professional realm.

Another CEO I met at DSA was Betty Kanelos. She owned a California-based lingerie company and asked if she could join our small group of CEOs that met twice a year, including Don Lovelace and Scott McKnight. We met at a resort for two days of exchanging ideas and inspiration. She became an important and inspiring part of the group. When she had some personal issues, she asked me to buy her company. That acquisition was very helpful in our expansion into California. This was another example of the power of partnering.

We began dropping products and converted Cameo to a pure party-plan business. The woman who did the first test party for me, Jeanie Denton, went on to become our top regional manager, replacing Kathleen Leinen who built her business selling bras. Jeanie stayed on top until she was replaced by Marlene Cain who then remained on top until we sold the business in 1999. She later played an important role in the turnaround of Wine Shop At Home.

Strategy: Training Is Crucial–Balance Work Information with Play–Listen to Consultant Challenges and Feedback while Building a Sense of Community

A direct sales company can grow only as fast as its sales force does, and a successful product is one whose unique features benefit from being explained. To do this in the most efficient manner, a team must be trained—so we consciously committed to training our teams intensively.

As the company evolved, so did our training methods. Our best program was Cameo's Regional School, which all new regionals attended. We based it on an idea borrowed from Mary Crowley of Home Interiors, who invited her top people to her vacation home in Colorado. Once a consultant reached the level of regional director, we invited them to a remote training retreat at the farm, beginning in 1984—though calling it a retreat was a little tongue in cheek, with twenty women sharing three bunk-style rooms and three bathrooms.

After paying their way to Dallas, John and I cooked for them and took care of everything for those five days at the ranch. Curriculum included a tour of the factory, product knowledge, recruiting, training, company policy, party plan, and marketing plan. Class days were eight hours long, but we also incorporated factory tours and plenty of recreation time for playing volleyball, relaxing in the hot tub, and riding horses. The ranch produced results. The ladies came in as strangers but left as family. They started independent but became interdependent, with a deeper sense of community. As Henry Van Dyke said, "[i]n the progress of personality, first comes a declaration of independence, and then a declaration of interdependence." One of the greatest benefits for us included the chance to listen to their challenges and get in-person feedback from them.

Philosophy: Create "Butterfly Habits" to Get to the Top

At Regional School, I gave the butterfly speech for the first time, and over the years, it became the school's graduation speech. I based it on a small book by Trina Paulus, *Hope for the Flower,* that shows a caterpillar's transformation to a cocoon and finally into a butterfly while telling the tale of two caterpillars on the journey. A parable about how we get to the top and make changes in our life, it illustrates the habits needed to be successful.

Wanting to become butterflies, two caterpillars decide to separate to find the way to the top. When the black caterpillar comes back as a butterfly, he chats with the yellow caterpillar. Following is my interpretation of their dialogue, which holds six secrets to becoming a great leader:

"How does one become a butterfly?" asked the yellow caterpillar.

"You must want to fly so much that you are willing to give up being a caterpillar."

"You mean to die?"

"Yes and no," said the black butterfly. "What looks like you will die, but what is really you will still live. Life is changed, not taken away. Isn't that different from those who die without ever becoming butterflies?"

Yellow decided to risk becoming a butterfly. She hung right outside the old cocoon and began to spin one of her own. "Imagine—I didn't even know I could do this. That is some encouragement that I am on the right track. If I have inside me the stuff to make cocoons, maybe the stuff of butterflies is there, too."

- **Imagine it.** The caterpillar had a vision. She imagined becoming a butterfly. Success comes by setting a goal. Goals are vision with a deadline. They tell us what we have achieved. As Ayn Rand said, "Achievement is man's highest moral purpose." To be motivating, goals need to be measurable and attainable. Goal setting can be a thoughtful, sometimes painful process. Making a daily to-do list is the simplest form of goal setting. You gain excitement as you mark items off. Andrew Carnegie is said to have paid a consultant twenty-five thousand dollars for that one idea during the Depression. That would be like paying $400k today.

- **Know why your cause is worth achieving.** Viktor Frankl, "If the why is strong enough, the how will come." When Pavlov was on his deathbed, his students asked the secret to his success. His reply? Passion and gradualness.

- **Believe in the dream.** Dreams are "long-term goals to overcome short-term failures." So dream the impossible dream—not just a wish but a *belief.* A dream without hope is just a wish, and a wish without belief is just a dream. Joan of Arc said, "I know this now. Every man gives his life for what he believes. Every woman gives her life for what she believes. Sometimes people believe in little or nothing, and so they give their lives for little or nothing. Leaders have a goal or a vision, and they give their life to it."

- **Courage.** The butterfly decided to hang by the old cocoon and spin one of her own. She knew she had to die if she was to become the butterfly she could be. The decision to fly, to achieve, to lead can be scary, but like Jack London, author of *White Fang,* said, "I would rather be ashes than dust! I would rather that my spark should burn out in a brilliant blaze than it should be stifled by dry-rot. I would rather be a superb meteor, every atom in me in magnificent glow, than a sleepy and permanent planet. The function of the man is to live, not to exist." Deciding to be a successful business builder and develop a downline can take lots of courage. Courage is not the absence of fear but, rather, the judgment that something else is more important. It's not fatalistic or self-destructive. As G. K. Chesterton said, "Courage is the willingness to die, taking the form of a strong desire to live."

Courage is not the absence of fear but, rather, the judgment that something else is more important.

- **Act on it.** Leaders are men and women of action. The caterpillar acted: she hung and began to spin. Execution is doing what is necessary to reach your goal. Being a successful leader means never giving up—because as James Michener said, "Character is what you do on the third and fourth try."
- **Focus.** Helen Keller said, "Losing your sight is not the worst thing that can happen—it's losing your vision." Like the butterfly said, "If I have inside me the stuff to make cocoons, maybe the stuff of butterflies is there, too." Nancy Austin, in *A Passion For Excellence* says, excitement comes with the first victory. If you believe in setting goals, you must believe in recognizing victories, including the small ones. Draw lines through your to-do list. According

to Oliver Wendell Holmes, "The great thing in this world is not so much where we stand, as in what direction we are moving." Earn your wings. Celebrate the small wins. The first success makes the rest possible. And if you have a larger long-range goal, you won't be frustrated by short-term failures (the cocoon). Learn from Renoir's explanation of how he could paint when even holding a brush caused him excruciating pain: "The pain passes; the beauty is forever."

Strategy: Create Products Consumers Want by Listening to Their Needs

We wanted to be not just *a* way to buy but *the* way to buy lingerie. To do that, we knew we had to uphold quality standards and create products the consumers wanted, which we could do by listening to their needs.

Christopher Morley said, "In every man's heart, there is a secret nerve that answers to the vibrations of beauty." A woman carries the vibration of beauty and is a work of art. Cameo's goal was to make women of all sizes feel confident and allow them to express their unique style in every mood or identity role. After all, even a Rembrandt looks better framed.

In 1981, Dr. Joyce Brothers, a psychiatrist, family life coach, and popular TV personality released the best selling book called *What Every Woman Should Know about Men*. In it, she offered advice about how men and women could improve communication to promote lasting love and happiness. She also wrote about a concept called "the total woman," noting multiple identities that span women's daily lives: wife, mother, and lover. Each identity could set a different tone and send a different communication signal.

And that's how we decided to design and sell lingerie. After successful market tests and playing on the information in Brothers's book, Cameo had expanded to include a variety of items in addition to bras. In the design process, we thought of women as a whole, respecting their individuality. Because every woman is unique, the line had to allow for individual and authentic expression.

In those days, you couldn't have gotten by with using a term like *mistress* as you probably could today. In any case, the term was Brothers's, not ours, so we modified the concept to make it our own, noting that women's moods and desires corresponded to the roles of wife, mother, and sweetheart, or lover. For instance: *Here's a soft, warm, and cuddly item when you want your husband to think of you as the mother of his children. Now, if you want him to think of you as his wife and the beautiful woman he married, you might want to wear something like this long, silky nightgown. And if you want him to think of you as his lover or—as some women might say—his mistress, here's this sexy, customized matching bra and panty set.*

Lingerie for the wife, the mother, and the lover

Over the years, our design team, along with many others, made our Cameo and Colesce brand world-famous. When Cameo expanded to Canada, the company rebranded as Colesce but would forever stay Cameo in many hearts. We were very fortunate to have developed a team that included professional designers, such as Mary Ann Hall; resource and supply chain experts, such as Michelle Duggett; and project professionals, such as Stephanie Gardner, who made sure our collections fit our philosophy and our customers.

One afternoon, while talking with Dr. Brothers and explaining our lingerie, design process, and sales strategy, I asked her, "What are your thoughts on this?"

"It's magnificent," she said.

"Would you be willing to do a show with us?" we asked.

She agreed. So we taped a show with Dr. Joyce Brothers, and in the show, she emphasized the wife, mother, and sweetheart story, noting that these roles and moods could be used to keep families together and marriages happy. We felt as if we were doing a great job, helping women have a better life.

Lesson: Persistence Pays

Cameo would dominate my business life for thirty years. For that segment of our life tree to thrive, we maximized our potential by developing two different, concurrent businesses at the same time. If we could achieve success with one business, then how about two? One business operated as a private-label bra business, and the other was the Cameo party-plan business. Essentially, we used our basic design but made cosmetic changes to differentiate it. Since I took care of the factories, I did most of the work on the private-label business by selling, signing franchises up, and gearing them to manufacture their product.

Some of the contracts took a little chasing, that bit of persistence that plays heavily into one's success. I once cold-called Jerry Brassfield, who was in direct selling with a company called Golden Products, to ask, "Would you be interested in adding this bra to your line of products?"

He said, "I'm having a meeting in Las Vegas next week. If you come out, we'll look at the bra and see what you have to say."

My brother and I flew to the meeting in Las Vegas. Every time we tried to see him though, he was busy. It was very discouraging, but we did end up talking to him—just briefly.

He said, "Well, I'm going to have another meeting in Chicago. Come up there, and I'll meet with you. We'll spend some time together. I'll have more time."

John and I went to Chicago to meet and were able to have a few more minutes there.

"This bra will be a great addition to your product line," I said, "because it makes a large woman appear smaller and a smaller woman appear larger, and you could sell it for ten dollars, a five time markup." I invited him to come to Oklahoma to see the factory and meet Brantley, the engineer, watch the product being made, and see it on a model: "Come see how we make it, and let's talk about it."

Since that's the kind of margin you need to have for a good direct-selling product, he perked up and flew down on a cold, bitter winter day. As we showed him through the factory, I said, "If we produce the bra in volume, a hundred thousand at a time, we can sell it as low as two dollars and retail it for ten dollars, which is the going price."

"Let me think about it," he said.

On the way back to Dallas, I drove into a blinding snowstorm and pulled off to the side of the road to let the storm pass. While sitting there, I kept talking to him about the bra.

"You know what," he said, "I think you're right. I'm going to do it."

"Well, I appreciate that. But the only way I can get started is if you can buy that hundred thousand."

"How much will I owe you?" he said.

"Two hundred thousand dollars," I said, and he pulled out a checkbook and wrote me a check for two hundred thousand dollars, sitting beside the road. Miraculously, it came at the perfect time to launch our private-label business and keep the factory running profitably.

Recently, on the interview series *The Legends of Direct Selling with over 50 Years in the Industry,* hosted by John Fleming in 2021, we were reunited. The group started introducing themselves, and I said, "Fellas, I don't know what I'm doing here. I'm just a poor boy from Waco, Texas, and I don't belong with you guys."

He interrupted and said, "You're so much more, Stan. You can't give us that stuff. Besides, you're the only guy I ever wrote a two hundred thousand dollar check to, sitting on the side of the road in a snowstorm."

We all had a good laugh—and as it turns out, most of us had had business dealings with each other over our fifty years. We sold Rick Goings, now

Chairman of Tupperware, premiums when he had a fire alarm business, Rudy Revak, now Chairman of Singular, sold those bras I sold to Jerry Brassfield at Golden Products, and I worked with John Fleming who ran a company that I asked to join the International Aloe Science Council.

In the early 1980s, we were selling skin care with our bras. The active ingredient was aloe vera. Several direct-selling companies were selling products that contained aloe vera but were getting frustrated with retailers who claimed aloe vera in their products. Investigation showed most only included a "fairy dusting" of aloe. Two of the members of our CEO group, Don Lovelace and Scott McKnight, and I talked about asking DSA to see if they could challenge this deception. They said their charter did not include product involvement and suggested we form an association to police it for us. I asked Jerry Gilbert, the DSA's outside counsel, to help us set it up. After he agreed, we asked Bob Brouse, the retired president of DSA to be our first executive director. I took on the job of recruiting members, and that's where I met Clint Howard of Carrington Labs and John Fleming of Sasco. We called it the National Aloe Science Council, and it serves the industry with distinction. We became inactive when we dropped aloe products from our line. Interestingly enough, the chief science officer of Carrington Labs later became the chief science officer of Mannatech.

Lesson: Never Assume You Completely Understand a Culture

The 1980s brought a lot of firsts, both personally and for the business. My first experience setting up a factory was when Cameo went international with the opening of Mexico in 1980, in partnership with Bob King and Guillermo Menendez. I traveled to Juarez, shipped the machinery from Oklahoma, and hired a local engineer to run the factory and manufacture the bra, which was that market's emphasis. Cameo later expanded to Canada, Thailand, Indonesia, Spain, and England, but one of our most notable cultural experiences happened in Indonesia.

We were working in Asia, where our partners, Bee Buranaphan and Pojanie, had built a wonderful business in Thailand, when a Time Life distributor proposed taking the bras to Indonesia. However, when he brought the idea up to us, it was with a bit of hesitancy: "The women are conservative, and they won't let you fit them in a bra. They won't let you touch them. You'll have to find some way of training without touching."

Excited at the prospect, I chose to look at the challenge as more of an opportunity and said, "Okay—I'll come over, see what we can come up with, and see if I can help you get started."

Once I arrived, they provided a model who agreed to be fitted into the bra. With the model standing next to me, I talked to the room of about fifty women. Bra in hand, I explained all the technical details and how awesome it was: "This bra is very unusual. It was designed by a helicopter designer to uplift the bust and keep them in the right position. To lift the bust and defy gravity, pull the bust through the triangle inside the bra and let it rest on the band that puts the weight on the back of the bra."

With the model properly fitted into the bra, the transformation became apparent, and to close the presentation, I said, "Well, that's it. And if you're interested in being able to sell this product, talk with Eddie."

Afterward, I'd thought I was through, but a woman came up and asked, "Would you mind fitting me in the bra?"

"Sure," I said, "if you're sure it's okay."

She looked around the room and said, "Let's go to the lady's restroom so nobody will know."

I carried my kit and measured the woman. When I put the Cameo bra on her, she was thrilled and looked at herself in the mirror with a sense of wonderment. But after I'd finished fitting her in the bra and walked out, almost every single woman in that room had lined up outside the restroom and wanted to be fitted, too. It was amazing. When I saw the line, I felt a sense of awe: Cameo seemed to defy limitations and cultural norms.

That's not to say that other challenges wouldn't arise from that expansion, though. Not because of the business but political militants began rioting in Jakarta and occupied the park outside our factory. Our operators couldn't even get into the building to make the product without entering through tunnels that connected the houses that lined the park. The business continued, but it never regained its momentum.

Strategy: Look for Opportunity in Market Trends—a Gain Can Be Attained in Loss

During the mid- to late-1980s, John and I added a couple branches to our business ventures. By the early 1980s, Texas banks had sustained large loan losses because of the savings and loan business and the drop in oil prices. This caused great banks like First National Bank and Republic Bank, two of the most important banks in the United States, to end up being taken over by the government. In a way, it was as if banks went on sale, and right about that time is when my longtime banker and friend, Jim Veers, approached me about another client of his who wanted to start a bank. Meeting Jim was serendipitous as we'd met when opening an account for Cameo, growing from being a new client and new business to having a substantial line of credit. Over the years of loans and throughout our business partnership, I'd joked with Jim and said, *"I sure would like to be on the other side of the banking desk."*

Well, he gave me that opportunity because his other client needed capital and salesmanship, which, after a small investment, led to my first foray into banking—and to becoming a board member of Texas Central Bank. I wasn't a large shareholder and never participated in the operations, but I served on the board of directors until it sold. Five years later, Art Ruff, the owner and founder of Texas Central, met with me about expanding my investment and buying more stock.

"You need to own more than 1,000 shares of stock," said Art.

"I don't have that kind of money," I said.

"Well, the bank will lend it to you, and you can pay it back. Don't worry, bank stock is good collateral for the loan," he said, with an insistent tone.

I took his knowing nudge, bought the stock, paid it off, and about a year later, Art announced he'd been diagnosed with cancer and needed to sell the bank. With that sale, my investment nearly quadrupled, and I still hold immense gratitude for his insistence then. So, from that point, I took the money in the banking kitty, so to speak, and parlayed the funds into additional banking ventures and partnerships. One investment led to the next and compounded the initial investment. Around the same time, we were contacted by another bank for help. John took that one on and ended up getting very involved. He eventually told me they needed more capital. Fortunately, I had the money from the bank sale and added to that money made from Cameo, resulting in 20 percent ownership of that bank.

All in all, I helped start, fund, or serve on the board of six different banks. And as for my time on the other side of the desk and approving loans, I think I had a keener understanding for the needs of new businesses, yet I was probably as tough as most bankers when deciding whether to lend somebody money.

The banking ventures continue to this day, and as they continue, they evolve, seemingly miles apart. Over time, I realized we may never know exactly the direction a business endeavor may head or how it will grow, but being open to its evolution as the world changes helps pay dividends.

★★★

While pursuing the banking interests, my primary focus continued to be on Cameo. And in 1989, a friend of mine passed away, who had been the CEO of a company called Queensway to Fashion, a big outerwear company and at one time the largest apparel party-plan company. Bob Williams, the new CEO, a guy I'd also met at a DSA meeting, asked me whether I wanted to take over the business. He did not want anything for it except a home for the consultants. I explained to him that the only way was if the salesforce would agree to it. We met with them, and thanks to leaders like Judy Kissey and Dixie Lee, they were convinced in spite of much opposition. We entered into an agreement, and all of a sudden, we

> # We may never know exactly the direction a business endeavor may head or how it will grow, but being open to its evolution as the world changes helps pay dividends.

were the owners of Queensway to Fashion, which was a great name and a very important addition to our business. We convinced Bob to move to Dallas and join us as vice president of sales promotion, a great addition to our team.

Our last major acquisition occurred just as we were selling the business. We had the opportunity to buy the iconic Multiples Brand outerwear business, brought to us by the CEO Katharine Gardner whom I'd been connected with at DSA board meetings. She had successfully transitioned the company from retail stores to a novel combination of Home Shopping Network and direct selling. We felt it would work well with Cameo/Colesce's loungewear line; however, the new owners eventually decided to discontinue it. Her involvement with the industry ultimately led Katharine to become founder of one of the premier search firms in the direct selling space, filling a real need for the industry.

Philosophy: Cast Your Bread on the Water

Dad had taught us to always give back some of what we made. If we didn't make anything, we could always be of service to the church, the poor, or the community. It could be more than 10 percent or less, depending on one's circumstances.

In my early years, most of my giving was through the church, and so was my service work. Later in life, after I served on the board of the National Paralysis Foundation, having taken George Bush's place when he resigned to run for governor, Mark Schank, chairman of the board of Professional Bank, asked me to serve on the development committee of Habitat for Humanity in addition to my roles with the Direct Selling Education Foundation and Baylor University's Center for Professional Selling.

At Mannatech, we created a foundation that was primarily funded by the associates donating a percentage of every sale to provide nutrition to malnourished children around the world. My son Landen, Mannatech's chief sales and marketing officer, added chairman of the board of the M5M Foundation to his duties. In 2019, we donated twenty million servings and in spite of Covid, in 2020, the foundation donated more than nine million servings to improve the health of children from six different countries. As a result, we have seen children make better grades, miss less school because of illness, and grow taller and stronger.

Instead of asking only what I can get from a situation, I was taught to ask, *"What can I do to help?"* That's probably why I wanted to become a teacher and preacher. A helpful heart and mission carried me through life and are built into the mission statement of Mannatech today. It's not something that we throw into a manual and forget about—it's a trait I've seen our leaders embody. I was so pleased when my son Stan, who is chairman of the board of Wine Shop At Home , selected America's

Mighty Warriors, a charitable foundation that provides support to Gold Star families, veterans, and their families, for their charitable efforts. For every bottle of Glory wine sold, two dollars is donated to the foundation, as well as a percentage of corporate profits. We think these methods of providing support are the best because it allows us to continue supporting even in difficult times.

While I was chairman of the Direct Selling Education Foundation during the late 1980s, we decided to create an award that recognized commitment to service. The board chose the name Circle of Honor because we saw the unending nature of the circle as a fitting symbol of the continuous and unending dependence that the foundation has on each honoree and of their unbroken commitment to the spirit of service.

A helpful heart and mission carried me through life and are built into the mission statement of Mannatech today.

We wanted the Circle of Honor award to be more than just an award—we wanted it to be a symbol. A symbol does not change; in a sense, it takes on a life all its own that allows it to mean much more than words or a mere award. Symbols are felt as well as understood. They speak to thirsty ears, and they resonate with hungry hearts. For the symbol aspect, we chose a hand-etched lead crystal cup that stands twelve inches tall on a walnut base, with lights illuminating the cup and its inscribed brass plate.

By its second year, the DSEF Circle of Honor was already becoming a recognized symbol of those who provided outstanding service to the foundation and who through their personal effort, energy, involvement, and support stood out above the rest. This was due in part to the first honorees, Bob Brouse and H. Thomas McGrath of Avon, who were essentially the founders of the DSEF and so worthy of the recognition.

Mary Kay Ash had been a major contributor to the foundation since its inception—and had made the first grant. In 1989, I had the honor of presenting her with the Circle of Honor Award.

Excerpt from Award Speech

"More and more women take their rightful place alongside men in business, education, and government. Throughout history, women have risen during times of great crisis to save races, countries, ideas, events, and industries to become symbols for others to follow. Esther saved the Hebrew race through courage and initiative. Cleopatra saved the nation of Egypt from Rome with her daring plans. Joan of Arc saved the French with her inspired faith. Marie Curie ensured the discovery of radiation. Florence Nightingale modernized healthcare. Susan Anthony inspired women's right to vote.

Washington Irving once said in *The Sketch Book,* "There is in every true woman's heart a spark of heavenly fire which lies dormant during the broad daylight of prosperity but which kindles up, and beams and blazes in the dark hour of adversity."

Mary Kay once sat on the back row at a Stanley Home Products Convention in Houston and was inspired to become not only the queen of sales for Stanley but the queen of direct selling by founding and building an international cosmetics company and leading it with charisma, candor, and character. Mary Kay, more than any other single individual, elevated the image of direct selling, increased earning opportunities for women, and set a personal standard of selflessness and integrity that inspired an industry."

Sales Lesson + Strategy: Mary Kay Ash—the Power of the Pen, Remembering Names, and Creating an Abundant Mind-set

Mary Kay was a legend in her own time. She never forgot a name and made time for handwritten thank-you cards. I am grateful for these lessons and methods, which helped mold our success in business and in the foundation. In her business, Mary Kay's awards were based on how consultants performed and how they helped others be successful. They weren't based solely on rank. I once asked her how a person became number one if they weren't first in sales or recruiting. She said, "Well, in our business, if we don't help other people do their job, we won't be able to get to where we want to go."

We began to develop some awards that were based on people being in competition with themselves rather than others. I believe that was the key to her philosophy—helping people understand that their success will be based on what they did, not what others did, with room for everyone to be number one. Such an approach creates a mind-set of abundance rather than scarcity.

The ability to network within an overarching industry organization, the DSA, greatly attributed to the success of our businesses. Though I'd been on its board of directors since 1980 and would serve on it until 2010, in 1988, while I was chairman, the industry was declining. Challenges brewed as sales declined. People were experiencing a tough time. As the dues fell off, the association lost money, and the expenses kept increasing. So I wondered *What would help the association stay afloat and sail to greater waters?*

My experience being fired from SMC Industries only reinforced the lesson that "everything will be okay in the end—and if it's not, then it's not the end." Success is never final. Failure is never fatal. If you start celebrating too soon, you might celebrate before the story is over—and only by mistaking a failure as the end does it become fatal.

To help offset the decline, we formed a blue-ribbon commission to study the organization in hopes of discovering what action was needed for a successful rebound. The number one recommendation was to increase the number of dues-paying members. We asked President Neil Offen to make that his primary responsibility and strongly recommended that the organization never be in a position where it didn't have the money to go on if a crisis happened or if members were lost and dues fell. The DSA needed some sort of backup—a sort of life preserver. We recommended the creation of a reserve account that saved up any year's surplus in a reserve fund, up to a maximum of 30 percent of the budget, to be able to meet any kind of crisis. The policy is still in effect today and has accumulated several million dollars, which carried us through several moments of crisis over the years.

The year 1988 was also the year I turned fifty. To celebrate, my wife threw a big party at the ranch, inviting our closest friends. I was amazed at how many people made the ninety-minute drive to help us celebrate. It was an all-day party with horseback riding, a watermelon seed–spitting contest, horseshoes, and barbecue capped off with country music and dancing. It was one of the most memorable events of my life. To feel the love and affection Judy showed to celebrate me, and the warmth and comradery of so many friends and partners joining us was a joyful event.

Just as I turned fifty and worked to close out the decade, the Direct Selling Association honored me with the Hall of Fame award. It was an exciting and humbling experience, bringing many emotions. Coming from my peers, the award was doubly significant. All my family attended, and I was given the chance to honor them. Without my wife and family's support and love—life's greatest beauty—I would never have been able to reach such a peak.

Jerry Heffel, CEO at Southwestern Books, Presenting 1989 Hall of Fame Award to J. Stanley Fredrick

Stan receiving DSEF circle of honor award from chairman of the board of MaryKay Inc.

CHAPTER 5

LISTEN TO DEMAND, THEN SELL IT

"If one advances confidently in the direction of his dreams, and endeavors to live the life which he has imagined, he will meet with a success unexpected in common hours."
Henry David Thoreau

Although life may have been flourishing in certain respects, other aspects presented more challenges and hence more opportunities. By the close of the 1980s, the price of beef had plummeted. We weren't making much money on cattle, and life on the ranch wasn't looking as prosperous. John and I began to brainstorm other avenues for turning it profitable, and we'd heard rumors of a new movement. Unknown to us at the time, for the following ten years, our attention would turn to a different animal.

America had joined the embargo of South Africa in the late 1980s over its policy of apartheid, so ostrich hides were no longer imported to be made into ostrich boots. The price of a pair of ostrich boots, if you could find them, rose from $150 to $800 or even $900. And then one enterprising Texas rancher said, "You know what? We ought to raise ostriches here."

John and I heard the rancher was importing them from Tanzania as chicks and thought it was a great idea. We started doing our own due diligence on raising ostriches. After looking into it some more, we found out that ostriches raised in South Africa were sheared for their feathers, which were sold for feather boas and feather dusters. Their feathers' little barbs make for dusters that pick up dust very well. We discovered that ostriches can also see for seven miles, so their eyes were used for research purposes. Additionally, Europeans, ate a lot of ostrich meat, which had a fine taste. Unlike most wild game, it did not have a wild taste—more like veal—and it had almost no fat or cholesterol. It sounded like a great meat business.

If we started raising ostriches, I figured we'd become pretty self-sufficient by selling the hides, various other parts, and the meat. However, the real opportunity turned out to be producing and selling trios to other ranchers who raised them to produce more ostriches and then sold them for their hides and meat. We developed a production business that was designed to raise ostriches. Eventually we had two incubators that could hatch five hundred eggs apiece, giving us more than a thousand ostriches running around our ranch.

We brought ostriches to the farm and paired them up to breed and lay eggs. By 1992, we built a five-thousand-square-foot ostrich barn that is now the home to the Blue Ostrich Winery, but then, we used it to incubate the eggs and house the chicks. We had pens with lots of trios—one male and two females. At first, we'd heard that the females would let a male have only one more female in the pen without getting mad, running the others off, or just plain fighting with them. Eventually we discovered that some breeds aren't monogamous at all and were . . . well, quite randy. Best of all, the females could carry five eggs in their tract at a time.

Lesson: Even a "Flightless Bird" Can See Soaring Success.[1]

At the time, most flights coming into Dallas arrived at Love Field. I'd ordered a couple pallets of month-old ostriches, and when they arrived, they were cute, furry animals that were just delightful. I'd arranged with a local rancher to raise them because he had the facilities needed to feed

---

[1] Ostriches are actually more akin to a dinosaur than a bird.

them every day and take care of them until they were old enough to move to the ranch.

When they were about six months old, he called me and said, "Well, they're ready to move."

"Okay," I said, "I'll come get them."

"Well, you oughta bring a lot of help because they aren't easy to handle."

"Those cute little guys? They were friendly."

"Just wait until you get here," he said.

I got there, and sure enough, they were meaner than snakes. Then I remembered that these birds were red ostriches from the wilds of Tanzania, and all had been laid in the wild before being gathered and hatched in captivity—direct descendants of wild animals that lived in the bush.

Just as I was taking in the rambunctious birds and considering how to handle them, the rancher said, "I'm going to get at the neck and pull on them. You get behind them and shove them."

"Hey," I said. "I don't get behind horses or cows."

But he assured me that ostriches can only kick forward, so I got behind the ostriches and we started loading them in my trailer. As he pulled them in, I pushed. After we loaded up, I took them to the ranch in Saint Jo, and that was the beginning of our ostrich business. That old rancher was right: for a good while, the ostrich business kicked forward and boomed—for most of the decade, in fact. At first we sold the ostriches when they were a year old, but the demand became so great that we started selling them when they were six months old and then only three months old. At three months old, a trio with two females and a male sold for five thousand dollars. It was absolutely amazing. One year, we took orders for over two million dollars in ostriches, which was more than we could produce; so, we had to return all those deposits.

That went on for about five years, and we made money hand over fist. It was a very lucrative business, but if life had taught me anything by then, it was that success is never final. Suddenly the market crashed, much as tulip mania had once done in Europe and chinchillas in the US. Eventually you could drive down country roads and come across ostriches that had been let loose. People couldn't sell them, and they couldn't take care of them anymore. We tried processing them for meat in Muenster at Fisher's Meat Market, but a three-hundred-pound ostrich produces only a hundred pounds of marketable meat, and only thirty pounds of that sold at a good price. For a little while, we sold Fredrick Ostrich Meats to fine dining restaurants like the Mansion, the Adolphus Hotel and The Crescent in Dallas, but soon the novelty wore off, and people started wanting their beef.

So we finally closed the business and sold the rest of the ostriches. Once we'd loaded them onto the trailer, about seven still didn't fit. The driver never returned to pick up those seven ostriches, so we fed and took care of them, out of sentiment. We called them "the lucky seven" and later used them as mascots for our wine business.

Blue Ostrich males once prized for producing hundreds of chicks
for our production business, now entertain Winery guests

Ranch house with herd of Black Angus and
mixed cattle grazing on Coastal Bermuda

The Farm

Stan Fredrick

The sun in Crayola gold
Hovers just above the hills.
It hangs on an invisible thread from the bow of an old oak
That stretches across the horizon,
To frame a photo for my memory.
In the pause before its plunge,
The farm is caught in perfect focus—
An old homestead with weathered paint,
Tattered screens, worn wood, and shattered windows,
Sags under the weight of use and years.
Yet stands its vigil over crumbling well,
Rusted plow, and horseless haywagon.
The bull nettle blooms as the bluebonnet fades,
And wild rye waves in the wind.
The last iris greets the first rose
While the fields yield green grasses,
And the hills thrive with cottonwood and oak.
Cattle are lowing in the distance,
A horse neighs, a lone quail calls,
And a butterfly hovers like a weightless feather
As the sun leaves a golden glow in the sky

★★★

Philosophy: Capitalism Is Critical for the Entrepreneurial Success and Spirit

I very much believe in the United States. Capitalism and the entrepreneurial spirit led to this country's success and laid the foundation for my own. Politics may have made it an unpopular opinion to some, but I firmly believe America is unique. It is special and has done something that no other country in modern times has. John wrote a nonfiction book about our ancestors who arrived here from Germany in 1799 and fought in the War of 1812 to defend their adopted country. They went on to farm five thousand acres, something impossible in their native country. And that's only the beginning—just stop and consider how many hardships people still go through to get to the United States in hope of gaining freedom and opportunity. Therefore, we were excited when the Berlin Wall fell. When Dad and my brother went over to see it, Dad brought back pieces of graffiti-painted rock he chipped from the wall.

John, Stan's dad, chipping off a piece of the Berlin Wall

After the Berlin Wall fell, I had the chance to experience a socialistic society on a visit to Russia, and I came home with a renewed belief in capitalism, something I still feel strongly about today. While I have erred on the side of caution with politics because the companies I'm involved with encompass more than 200,000 associates around the world, I think it's important that people know that I am very conservative in my political beliefs. Current events in America are a move toward socialism and communism, which I believe to be a real danger to the country.

In about 1990, someone came to me and said he'd been contacted by the Russian Department of Television. They were wanting to go into different businesses, and one they were hoping to expand into was sewing factories making lingerie because Russian women had very little choice in lingerie.

"I'll be glad to talk to them," I said, so I flew over to talk to the Ministry of Television's representative and his crew. When I landed at Saint Petersburg International Airport, I scanned the area for the lights of the terminal. It was a dark, snowy night, and when we pulled up, I finally saw a naked light bulb hanging from a post in the distance. The plane parked on the tarmac, and I walked through the snow to the terminal to go inside. As it turned out, the naked bulb was the terminal. I went inside and it was all open air—no difference between the temperature outside and inside.

Before I'd left, I'd been told not to bring any money with me because it would be confiscated: if I chose to bring some money, I'd need to hide it. So I stuffed six thousand dollars into my cowboy boot. After I got my luggage, I started wondering where I could find a currency exchange. The people didn't speak my language, and I didn't speak theirs. I started to feel helpless and became increasingly worried about the money I'd smuggled in my boot.

I finally met my contact at the Europa Hotel where I was staying, and he said, "We don't want you to stay in the nice hotels. The Europa is the best hotel in town, but we don't want you to stay here. We want you to experience life as someone who lives here would."

They set up a "nice" apartment house for me. My apartment was one room, about twenty by twenty feet, with a stove, a toilet, and a sink with running water. Just as I was settling in, they said, "Don't drink the water out of the tap. We have bottled water for you."

"Okay, I'm thirsty now. Do you have some water you can bring me?" "Tomorrow. Tomorrow, we bring you water."

Based on looks alone, nobody in their right mind would live here. Trying not to be insulting, I acted as if it were okay.

The next morning, I got up and asked for bottled water.

"Not today. Tomorrow morning, you'll have water."

I got some bottled water in town, which solved the problem. After a week, the promised water had still not arrived. Apparently it was considered unpatriotic to admit there was a shortage. But I still needed to find somewhere to exchange currency, so I asked my guide, "Is there a currency exchange where I can change some money?"

"If you take that money to a currency exchange, they won't give you anything for it."

"Okay, what do I do?"

"I know a guy," he said.

He took me into a deep, dark area of St. Petersburg, and as I was about to get out of the vehicle, he said, "No, you'll have to wait in the car. Give me the money, and I'll take care of it."

I gave him a thousand dollars. He went away and came back in a minute. He gave me the rubles at a reasonable exchange rate. The official exchange rate at the time was six rubles to the dollar, but on the black market it was three hundred to one—inflation was that bad.

I'd never seen any place so bleak and desolate in my life. When I went to the store to see what kind of products the competition had, I was shocked to see that the store shelves were completely bare. Only one or two pieces hung in the lingerie section; in the shoe department, only one or two pairs of shoes. Little old women cleared the streets of snow, using wooden shovels.

One day, they took me to lunch. We had a sandwich, a coffee, and a dessert for seventy-five cents. While I was eating, I couldn't help but ask myself *How in the world are they making all that for seventy-five cents?* But then I realized the average worker would need 225 rubles to buy it, more like a day's wages. Later that same day, we went to the Europa for dinner. There, the same meal we'd had at lunch cost twenty dollars. The difference in prices between where the rich and the poor—or even the average—shopped was shocking.

When we eventually found someone who wanted to be a distributor, we cautioned that the first thing to do would be to set up a distributorship, to find out whether the products would sell in Russia before launching production.

When I was preparing to leave, trying to figure out where to go and what to do at the airport—still with that money in my boots—somebody scowled at me and said, "Passport and documents."

"Documents? I don't understand documents."

"You need documents to leave the country," he said.

I looked around and saw a table with a few people standing and waiting. Nobody was saying a word as if they were all afraid. The room was deathly silent. The man started getting frustrated with me, so figuring that maybe they'd given me something when I came in, I pulled out all my papers in a sheaf and handed them to him. "Finally," he said, and pulled out the one he needed.

"Where do I go now?"

Without a word, he pointed across the room at a door in the distance. The room was like a gymnasium, and crossing it felt like crossing no man's land. As I walked, I thought he seemed increasingly suspicious of me. *He's going to come get me. They're going to search me, and they're going to find that money. And then I'm going to be arrested as a smuggler and go to prison.*

Sweating as my cowboy boots clomped across the floor, I suddenly heard steps behind me. *Oh, my gosh, they're coming to get me.* My mind raced as the steps got faster. My heart pounded. *Don't look back, don't look back.* The door seemed like it was getting farther away. *Maybe I can get there before he gets me.*

Nervously reaching for the door, I opened it and went in. No one followed me. I walked into a large room where lots of people were laughing, talking, and having a great time. I remember thinking, *Wow, you can tell it's the free world on this side.*

Initially, our products sold really well. But soon, our distributor told us he could no longer be our distributor: the Russian mafia had bolted his door closed, and he couldn't get in. The last shipment of products we'd shipped over had been confiscated. He would help us if we wanted to fight it, he said, but he warned us that the people were ruthless and didn't want us there. They wanted to do it themselves. There were plenty of other countries to work on, so we just let it go. The difference between communism and capitalism was very apparent.

After my experience with a socialistic society, to see America progress in that direction is a bit frightening. I remember all too well how joyously people all over the world reacted to the fall of the Berlin Wall. Yet here we are thirty years later, and people cannot remember why they were so happy. In fact, the ones who rejoiced are probably not with us anymore, and a whole new generation has grown up, not knowing the horrors of communism, the failures of socialism, or the liberating qualities of free enterprise and capitalism.

Lesson: Know Your Customer–across Continents

One of my travel adventures taught me a marketing lesson and gave me a humbling and unforgettable experience. I had designed a girdle that was like a panty girdle. Most girdles tended to make a woman's rear end look flat, so when we molded cups in the back to keep its natural shape, our saleswomen called it a "fanny bra" because it lifted and shaped the derrière just like a bra did for the bust. We felt really good about it, and it was selling like hotcakes in the States.

Our organization in England wanted me to introduce it there, so after being introduced professionally and politely, I stood in front of a group of fifteen women and started chatting. Finally, I got to the bras and said, "Now, I want to show you this brand new—you're the first in England to see this—fanny bra." These women, who had been looking at me in adoration, suddenly dropped their eyes and bowed their heads. I kept talking about how the fanny bra would do wonders for them, but they weren't looking at me. They were looking at the floor.

I looked over at the manager, who'd become a good friend, and asked, "What's happening?"

She came over and whispered to me, "I should have told you, but in England, *fanny* isn't the derrière—it's the . . . front."

I could have crawled under the table. I apologized and apologized, and after a while they started looking at me again. It might have been the most embarrassing moment of my life—certainly it took some time and effort to regain their good graces.

Lesson: Timing Is Everything

Around 1992, some investment banker friends invited John and me to a casual meeting. After catching up on our families and investments, they said, "You're the perfect candidate to be a public company. We'd like to take Cameo public." I started weighing the pros and cons in my mind as they continued: Raising capital for expansion was easier as a public company. It also gave us an exit strategy and a way to monetize our investment. In my opinion, though, going public brought more disadvantages than advantages.

"We could sell a minority interest, make you a public company, and put a lot of money in your pocket too," they said.

At this point, Cameo had been in business twenty-five years. We didn't need the capital, and we weren't looking for an exit strategy. We had too many women depending on us, so going public wasn't really something that I was enthusiastic about.

"I'm not excited about going public," I said, "but John and I talked about it, and if they think it's the thing to do, and really recommend it, maybe we should do it."

Shortly after, we started the process and put together the S-1 documentation, the detailed prospectus for the company to go public. By the time we were ready to go on the stock market, they'd priced it at twelve dollars a share, which would make us enough money for it all to seem worthwhile. They'd even set the time we would go public.

A couple of days before we were to go public, some kind of catastrophe hit the market. The stock market plunged. Stocks plunged. Initial Public Offerings (IPOs) were being canceled. People weren't going public. Our investment friends came back and said, "We can go, but the best we could hope for is six dollars a share. We recommend that you not go public."

After that, the handwriting seemed to be on the wall: we shouldn't go public at all. So we paid our lawyer handsomely for the process and decided to stay a private company. Although it had been stressful at times, it was still a fun process and a learning experience.

Lesson: Listen to the Demand, Then Supply It

We'd started with one woman in 1970, and by 1991, we had twenty-eight thousand consultants in the United States. Our first factory had seventeen operators, and we'd added two additional factories in the United States and had over 500 operators. The original factory in Frederick, Oklahoma, was run by Dick Dickerson, a sewing machine mechanic whom we promoted to plant manager where he excelled at production and quality control. We opened another plant in Muenster, Texas, because of a dress factory plant manager named Bernice Sicking who said she would run the plant for us if we brought it to town. She turned out to be the best moneymaker I had ever seen as a plant manager. In our search for more production, we found a factory in Ogden, Utah, owned by a brilliant production manager who agreed to sell us the plant and stay on as the manager. Gary Pilkington, the manager, became our highest volume producer. As always, it was the right people who made the difference.

When we sold Cameo/Colesce in 1999, the guy who had purchased it had a bra he liked better than ours—but the customers who bought our product were very loyal over the years. Some people have been selling our bra since the beginning, such as Barbara Paine, Vondel Reynolds, Kathleen Leinen, and Sandy Anderson. They're a bit older now, but they still have people calling them for bras. The salespeople called me in a frenzy and said, "He's going to stop selling this bra. You need to make it available somehow. How can you make it available?"

Luckily, we had a franchisee in Thailand selling the product, so I asked them to make it for us and created what we call Custom Fit Bra Company today. I asked my son, Stan II, to set it up and run it for us. As a great leader and executive, he knew most of the distributors; he had worked with Cameo since college and had worked his way up to senior vice president. He'd even opened up Canada for us. Stan II and Aline Robert built it to a ten-million-dollar business in a just a few years.

Jamie, who now runs Custom Fit Bra Company, graduated from ACU with a degree in drama, but instead of acting or teaching, she decided to follow me into business. From the beginning, she was a determined, tenacious worker who could sell, recruit, and organize. She helped me fix several different departments before starting a career in retailing. She quickly rose to regional manager and worked until starting a family by adopting a friend's baby since she could not have one of her own. In 2015, when we needed someone to take over the Custom Fit Bra Company, I asked Jamie if she was ready to go back to work. She took over the business as if she had never been gone. The business has since prospered under her leadership in spite of embargoes, supply chain issues, and pandemics.

Jamie, third child and second daughter

All my life, we did everything together. We worked together, played together, got into trouble together–and learned to depend on each other.

The house where we grew up had a lot of oak trees. In the fall, when the leaves fell, we were always raking leaves–it was a big job. Dad made every job fun or turned it into a money-making enterprise. For this one, we made ten cents a bag, raking the leaves and putting them in a bag. Of course, first we jumped in them and played.

One particular Saturday in elementary or middle school, though, I had a paper to write. Although Saturday was raking day, Dad said, "You can't come. You have to do your paper."

So I sat in our game room and looked out the big glass windows, watching everyone working while I did my paper. I worked for a while, probably a couple hours, until I couldn't take it any more. I begged, "Please, Dad, please, can I rake? I don't even want ten cents a bag. I just want to rake leaves."

It might sound crazy that all I wanted to do was be outside raking leaves, but really all I wanted to do was be with everybody. Dad taught us how to be together and work as a team while making it fun. It's one of my favorite memories of being together, and it taught me that work doesn't have to be work—work can be fun.

★ ★ ★

With the end of the millennium drawing near, life seemed to be pointing to the end of a business era with my brother. In the mid-1990s, John had his first heart attack. When he had a tough time of it and underwent bypass surgery in 1997, it became clear to us that his involvement would lessen. Because of his poor health, it was time to sell the banks and lighten his load. Yet, with the dot-coms bursting, the stock market dropping, and the fear of the new millennium, it did not appear to be the right time to sell.

However, we did very well with that sale. Banks usually sell for about two times book, but Irving National sold for almost three times. One of the men who helped make that happen was a board member named Larry Jobe whom I later asked to serve on Mannatech's board and chair our audit committee. Larry later founded a new bank, Independent Bank of Irving. John and I both invested with him.

About the same time, my old friend and banker Jim Veers asked me if I would be a founding board member of Jack Siefrick's proposed bank, Professional Community Bank. I met Jack, a Harvard graduate, a CPA, and an astute businessman, and liked him personally and admired his vision. Jack persuaded Jamie Miller, a very successful banker, to take over as president and Mark Schank, a well-known lawyer and board member, to take over as chairman. Professional Community Bank was very successful, creating two strong branches under the leadership of Mark Smith and Jamie Miller, the president. After several years of solid growth, he sold the bank to Veritex Bank for almost two times book, who changed their mission to growth over community.

At this time, Larry needed capital for Independent Bank. So, I was faced with a dilemma: *do I retire from banking or jump back in with all of "my winnings"?* Having a lot of faith in Larry and his board, I went "all in," including going on the board. Our growth was spurred by a strategic planning meeting with Tony Jeary that allowed Larry to make a strategic sale to Veritex, the same bank we had sold Professional Bank to. Larry made a good deal with Veritex, which became a great deal when the stock went from twelve dollars to twenty-six dollars. All of this started with using the $10,000 from direct selling to buy stock in a bank. This was another great example of things working out in the end.

When the stock John and I received in the sale of Irving National Bank more than doubled in less than a year, my financial advisor advised us to sell most of it and diversify. My wife and I thought this prudent, but my brother decided to keep his in the bank stock even after I and his son, John Jr., encouraged him to diversify. John believed in putting all his eggs in one basket—*and then watching that basket*. This worked out well for him in the beginning, but in 2008, when the banks collapsed, his stock lost most of its value. He turned what was left over to a financial advisor, and he was able to retire and comfortably enjoy the ranch, as he had always planned.

CHAPTER 6
MAINTAIN A WORK-LIFE BALANCE

"We are made to persist. That's how we find out who we are."
Tobias Wolff

Strategy: You Cover More Ground Working with Partners

My little brother, Craig, had always been a fun little brother. He always looked up to his big brothers, especially John, and we had been good friends and good buddies. Dad seemed to have more time to enjoy Craig than he had with John or me. They really enjoyed fishing together, which John and I did not have the patience for.

Craig grasps things quickly—he is actually the smartest of us three. He'd always been very much an entrepreneur and had multiple business ventures of his own. We were close and enjoyed being together, and in terms of the Cameo business, he worked for us when he got out of the Navy for a while, but he really wanted to do his own thing.

He'd been doing really well with a trucking and shipping business we helped him start, and when the unions came to unionize him, he told them where they could put their union cards. When they told him how accidents and other bad things happen to people who aren't members of the union, he told them he wasn't going to be bullied and threw them out. A few weeks later, he went out to start the trucks and found that none of them would start. Turns out all of them appeared to have sugar in their gas tanks, which had completely ruined the engines. So he closed the business, vowing to start over. He had that family trait that knew it was only failure if you never try again.

Around the time John and I were winding down some of our business deals, Craig came to us and asked for our help getting into a business again. We agreed and pretty soon, he found a company, Weldon, that did truck conversions. They took four-door trucks with a sleeper cabin on them and cut them down into day trucks. If someone needed a sleeper on a truck, Weldon could add it on. He even ended up making a deal with Peterbilt to convert their two-door trucks to four doors. It was an interesting business, and we helped him buy it; he still has it today. We put up the money and took a royalty for doing so, structuring the deal so that he owned the business himself, and we owned the real estate. All his persistence paid off as it turned out to be very profitable for both of us.

A portrait of the Fredrick family

While Craig enjoyed fishing, hunting was more of my thing. Ever since shooting my first deer with Dad's Model 94 Winchester 3030, we'd talked about going big game hunting. It wasn't until the seventies that I had the opportunity to do so. Carl McAfee, a friend from Central Church of Christ moved to Montana and invited John and me to go elk, antelope, and deer hunting. In the beginning, it was just the two of us, but after seeing how the experience and operation worked, our boys and dad joined the next year.

The next year in the Lewis and Clark Forest, we parked the truck and entered the mountains. After walking for miles, we found a perfect place and shot three deer—and then it dawned on us, we were twenty miles deep in the wilderness with no horses and no truck to carry three field-dressed deer back to civilization.

Improvising, we took a big, long pole from a fallen tree, knocking the limbs off of it and tied the deer to three different places. John and I pushed from the inside and the boys from the outside until we dragged those deer back to the truck, having to stop several times along the way. Looking back, it may have not been a full twenty miles, but it definitely felt like it and was the hardest I've ever worked to get meat on the table.

In the early eighties, a friend from Colorado invited us to experience big game hunting and to learn how to hunt elk, a very exciting process. Our friend and guide was a former sergeant in the army, and although he was a policeman at the time, he still acted like a sergeant and had adapted some of the techniques learned during his service, particularly hunting as a team. On one of our first trips with him, he pointed at a map said, "This mountain is where we are going to hunt. You guys are the pushers and will hike up, spread out across the mountain, and walk down. The pointers will then be in position at the bottom of the mountain to shoot what you don't shoot on the way down."

It sounded easy, yet the walk up was a killer. The walk across was not bad, but the walk down was treacherous. Hunting turned out to be hard work, yet it turned out to be worth it.

Covering more ground as a team always proved to be an amazing method for hunting. We'd always "tag out" and have elk hanging all over the campground. A favorite memory from the entire time spent hunting was the last year Dad went with us. Seeing him at ninety-two years old, sleeping in a tent, and riding on horseback at 11,000 feet in the snow with a Model 243 replacing that Model 94 strapped to his back was incredible. His strength amazed me then, and I continue to draw on it for inspiration today.

Stan II, second child and first son

"For twenty-five years, Dad and I hunted together in Montana and Colorado with my grandfather, Uncle John, cousin John Jr. and a group of about eight other friends. For many of those, we slept in a rustic cabin on a river in a beautiful valley south of Gunnison, Colorado. It was a wonderful time of bonding and enjoying God's creation.

Of all the great hunting adventures during those years and the many great stories, the event that is burned into my memory more than any other was the year I had the most incredible migraine headache, probably from the altitude. I had never felt anything like it before or since. Dad saw me laying on the sofa, rubbing my temples with tears in my eyes, and immediately came over and began rubbing them for me. Dad has these big strong hands, and although it didn't take the pain away immediately, it was incredibly soothing and comforting. But it wasn't just that it felt good or even that Dad took the time to do it, it's that he knelt at the end of that couch and rubbed my temples for what seemed, and may have been, hours. Not just once, but several times over the two days it persisted. Perhaps it was because of the pain, but it was the most selfless act I had ever experienced toward me from anyone.

In my life since then, anytime my wife, kids, or anyone else for that matter asks me to do something for them and I don't feel like it doing it, I think of that moment and ask myself, *"What would Dad do?"* Dad has always been selfless that way. I've seen it with all of my siblings and especially with my mother."

Philosophy: Those Who Love the Lord Will Make Things Work Out

A popular scripture says, "All things work together for good for those who love the Lord" (Rom. 8:28)—although I understand the original Greek actually translates to "Those who love the Lord will make things work out."

My philosophy is that any time you face a problem, if you just can realize that it's going to work out—that you're going to solve it *somehow*—it will eventually work out for you. As the saying goes, "Everything works out in the end—if not, then it's not the end yet."

Even when things have looked really bad for a while, somehow they've worked out. If I could tell people anything, it would be about that Bible verse. I think people often misquote it or misunderstand its meaning. There's a big difference between sitting and waiting for God to reach down because you think He is going to make it work out for you, or using a godly spirit to find ways of making things work out. That's how I've tried to live my life, although I give my wife a lot of the credit. My confidence, certainty, and energy increased after I married her. She was very accepting, like my parents, and I loved how she supported everything I tried to do. Choosing a good partner for life, as in business, can make all the difference.

Philosophy: You Can Want Something, and You Can Look for It, but in the End, You Have to Go for It

Another thing I believe in strongly is Jesus's teaching about asking, seeking, and finding: "Ask and it will be given to you. Seek and you will find; knock and it will be open to you" (Matt. 7:7). I've always told our distributors that you can want something, and you can look for it, but in the end, you have to go for it. You have to knock. I think that's what Jesus was saying: until you knock, it's not going to open to you—taking action and making it happen is the real secret.

I say all this because at the start of the twenty-first century, I found myself seeking again and re-reckoning with retirement. At the time, I'd felt I could retire. I had remembered that one of my goals had always been to not worry about whether we'd have enough money to pay our bills. It was really something to know that we didn't have to worry about money anymore or even about going to work. I knew I didn't *need* to work anymore. Was this what retirement felt like?

A strangely peaceful feeling came over me. All my years, although I'd had a calm way of dealing with life, things had always run through my head—things that needed to be done, tasks that needed to be completed. Then one day someone asked what I was doing, and I said, "I retired."

After that, I began to notice how people treated the retired. One day we were out with Judy's brothers and sisters, who were all older and had retired. We went to a restaurant, and while sitting around having breakfast, the waitress started treating us shabbily, like we were toddlers. Judy's family was full of brilliant, strong businesspeople, one of whom even had a PhD, yet the waitress seemed to see us as if we didn't have any sense. We wouldn't have been treated that way in a business meeting! I decided then that if that was how retired people were treated, I didn't want to be a retired person, and since then I've never called myself retired. Interestingly enough, less than six months afterward, the opportunity to buy into Mannatech came along, and I was ready "to knock."

Strategy: Use the Proven Warren Buffett Method When Investing

Warren Buffett, the most successful investor of our time, has described his philosophy of investing as buying in a growing industry, buying a growing company, and holding for the long term. So when Bob King, the former CEO of World Book, who had taken me under his wing at the Direct Selling Association and had since become a consultant to the industry, introduced me to Mannatech and told me they were looking for a "white knight"—someone to buy out a dissident shareholder who was dumping his shares on the stock market—I decided to look into the supplement company, albeit with a little hesitancy.

As a member of the DSA board, I was well aware that companies don't always last, and I knew of federal and state efforts to outlaw or control companies. To be frank, I also had no interest in buying into nutrition; I'd previously bought a company that sold nutrition products, without much success. Talking with the CEO and then with one of the founders, Sam Caster, we discussed the product, plan, and vision. Thousands of associates were building businesses and providing nutrition to people around the world. It was exciting to hear how well-accepted the products were and about the initiative taken by the associates. Many of the associates had moved from the US to places like Australia, South Africa, Japan, and Korea to take the products to those countries, which showed a real and tremendous belief in the business.

Many planted seeds then that continue to grow today like Ji-Man Jung, our number-one associate in Korea, who was followed by Soo-Kyung Kim. They were followed by the star council members Young-Su Kang and Myong-Jin Lee. Just as powerful were Chang-Sun Kim, Jeong-Min Shin, and Sin-Ae Bae. This team is now being led to new records by Jay Roh, the general manager of Korea.

In South Africa, Louis and Leone Van de Linde started the business, resulting in the development of two top associates, Vincent Van der Linde and JP Koster, who continue to be supported and reach new heights by Manager Darren Hoffman.

Canadian leaders Julia Zhu and Tony Bao urged us to open China, resulting in our expansion into Hong Kong. Hanson Ma followed their lead to drive continued growth in Hong Kong under the leadership of the general manager of greater China, Tim Chang. They continue to see explosive growth today.

The co-founder Ray Robbins, who brought most of the initial sales-force to the company in the beginning, was a hardworking, charismatic leader and one of the best recruiters I've ever met. He was excited about my buying out the dissident shareholder since he was such a negative influence in the field, and I was thrilled to be associated with such a strong recruiter.

This team continues to plant the seeds of success, living up to the old Chinese proverb: *the best time to plant a tree is twenty years ago. The next best time is today.* This group of quality leaders and the ones who continue to lead our international expansion, such as Chris Simons, our regional president, helped inspire me to make that original investment and continue to fuel my belief today.

Ray Robbins, Mannatech cofounder

"Stan is like a brother to me and has taught me so much. He delights in the successes of other people and has an attitude toward everyone that most people have toward their family. He's family-oriented, but it goes beyond that. He has a natural desire to make everyone around him have a better life and have more success, happiness, joy, and purpose.

I've learned from him, probably more than anyone else, to make sure you stay within your profit margin. Don't spend money that is going to keep you from staying profitable. You can spend a lot but not to the point of consistently taking a loss. He taught me to spend money on incentivizing staff and to make sure they have a bonus structure that is very good if they do very good things. Basically, don't spend money that might get you in trouble, but always spend money that would benefit people who are making the business happen for you.

Stan has always been a salesperson at heart. He always thinks of the sales associate because he has always been a salesperson and knows that the salesperson is the most important part of any organization."

Stan and Ray Robbins

The Mannatech products, which were scientific, valid, patented, and proprietary, appealed to me, as did the earning opportunity and the low cost of entry for consultants. It was my first experience with a network marketing compensation plan. People were making a lot of money, and they believed in using the product themselves. I loved the fact that your customers could be your distributors, and your distributors could be your customers. That means, a distributor could make a referral fee on a customer, and a customer could make a referral fee on another customer. My interest grew beyond my prior experiences, and I began to look at it as a long-term investment.

The two major enemies of man are disease and poverty. Millions lost jobs when the dot-com bubble burst, but I believed that this method of selling could help bridge the gap between poverty and prosperity. The answer to disease was embracing wellness: the natural search for the fountain of youth and the loss of faith in traditional medicine. Those who are not in poverty wish to improve their quality of life, and with the wellness industry on the rise and the direct-selling method of distribution—which they called network marketing—growing faster than retail and mail order,

Mannatech offered a potential resolution for both. The company had built a record of explosive growth until it had experienced some internal problems, though that had nothing to do with its fundamental business. I saw the opportunity for the company to grow.

Yet the business had been declining. At the time, a few months after our bank sale, Mannatech's stock had declined from twenty-two dollars to two dollars a share. During the negotiations, while offering to buy the shareholder's interest, I told the CEO, "I'll only do it if you put me on the board and pay me a consultant fee."

The CEO wasn't too happy about that, but it was a good deal for the company, which would get rid of an unhappy partner who made a substantial salary and was dumping his shares and pushing the share price down. I could write a check for an amount few people could, and those who could weren't crazy enough, as some saw it, to buy when the price was declining every day.

Always spend money that would benefit people who are making the business happen for you.

"If you keep waiting," I said, "the stock is going to go to zero. At least this way you salvage some of your investment."

Between the time we'd agreed on a deal and the time we planned to close, the September 11 attack occurred. Everything crashed around us, and many thought I was lucky and would come to my senses. I didn't have to write the check—I could have backed out. There was nothing keeping me from doing so, but I felt confident John would want to partner and I would not have to share the burden alone. In the end, he backed out, leaving it to me to make a lone decision. Greater than the fear of loss was my belief in the product and the appeal of being a large shareholder. So I wrote the check and became the second-largest shareholder.

Although I'd joined the board and was a paid consultant, the CEO refused to give me an office in the building. He wouldn't listen to counsel or accept suggestions, which was surprising, considering my forty-five years in the industry, besides being a major shareholder and board member. It seemed strange that suddenly the "white knight" had become his enemy.

Despite the conflicting and fearful nature of the CEO, in two years, we made some major progress in reorganization. In 2002, when there was a vacancy on the board, I nominated Alan Kennedy, the former president of Nature's Sunshine, who had been in the industry for thirty years and was already a legend in the industry. There was no way they could turn him down. In 2003, I nominated Jerry Gilbert, the former outside counsel to DSA for thirty years who mentored me as I learned the nuances of board membership and the protocols of board leadership, and Pat Weir, the former president of Encyclopedia Britannica who had helped me with the Blue Ribbon Commission to reorganize DSA.

We also followed the industry example and invited our number-one associate and Platinum Presidential distributor, Ray Robbins, to serve on the board. When he retired, we asked his son Kevin, a Silver Presidential distributor, to replace him. Both of whom have served with distinction.

Kevin Robbins, Mannatech board member

"Stan Fredrick is a man of character, integrity, and ethics. When I first met Stan, just after he had become the largest shareholder in Mannatech, I was a little skeptical. He told me that he loved the product line and intended to hold onto the shares and make this a long-term, family investment. Twenty years later, Stan Fredrick has been a man of his word.

Stan Fredrick believes passionately in the direct-sales model. He believes in the power of the entrepreneur with a dream."

All of these new, independent board members were surprised I'd nominated them because we didn't always agree on industry or association issues. Over the years, being ready for opportunity was a big part of success as well as preparation, asking questions, and listening to the other side to understand their rationale. During our interactions at DSA meetings, I felt so strongly about protecting the industry that I was willing to challenge the association executives from a financial operating standpoint. I was very pleased with their reaction, their willingness to listen, and their preparation that I remembered it years later. Many have commented to me that they appreciated my willingness to consistently ask questions, which brought up issues that everybody was thinking and wanting to ask about but were just too reticent. The industry was too important for me to not voice my concerns and ask questions, so my feeling is, if you agree to serve, study the materials so you can ask serious questions.

Jerry, Allan, and Pat were smart leaders and partners, and the four of us became a strong force and decided to replace the CEO.

"Who's going to be the CEO? Are you going to be?" they asked.

"Absolutely not," I said. "I'm not at that stage in my life."

So that same year, we asked Sam Caster to be CEO and chairman. He wasn't a detail type of person and didn't like doing many CEO and chairman duties—he thrived more on the sales end. A new position had become popular among corporations when the head of the company was the CEO and chairman, and the board had put me in this role, called Lead Director. I handled all meetings, attendees, and agendas, helping the CEO with business issues, like an executive chairman would.

By this point, my belief in the products and the strength of the company had only grown, reinforced by my wife's experience. Judy had a condition that affected her salivary and tear glands. It gave her dry eyes and a dry mouth but also affected her kidneys; her nephrologist said she'd soon have to go on dialysis. She'd been taking a chemotherapy drug, called Imuran, and prednisone, causing her to gain weight and to have a miserable quality of life. After we invested in the company, she started taking Ambrotose Complex, and within two years, she had progressed to where she was exulting in the liberation she experienced while integrating nutrition with her nephrologist-recommended protocol. She began living the life she'd once dreamed about.

Judy, wife

"Stan came home one day and said, 'I just found a company we're going to invest in. It's going to make us comfortable, and it's going to help you get your life back.'

I said, 'Sounds wonderful. What is it?'

I soon started taking the product and was diligent about not missing a day. My quality of life improved dramatically. I was now giving my body what it needed, the nutrition it was missing, along with my doctor's regimen. About two years later, when my kidney doctor left his report in the room and he stepped out for a minute, I read it: *She has been taking this product, which she thinks has helped her, and her numbers are getting better.*

I took that as him being a little convinced that what I was taking was doing the job. It's been all these years, and I'm still taking Ambrotose every day and benefiting from the impact it has had on my quality of life."

Stan and Judy in front of the Christmas tree

Business was booming, and in 2006, with Sam as CEO and me as lead director, the company did more than four hundred million dollars in sales with more than a million distributors. We felt good about this, especially since we were not getting any complaints from our customers or distributors. We checked and the Federal Trade Commission had only had sixteen complaints, all about minor things like a backorder or a replacement. Nobody had complained about losing money. Nobody had complained about any adverse events. The complaints were so minor that the FTC didn't even notify us.

A lot of people followed our stock, and since the time of my investment, it had gone from a dollar per share to twenty-six dollars per share. You can imagine our shock when, out of the blue, *Barron's* published articles about our company that painted it in a negative light. After their two-page feature, the stock dropped to twelve dollars before bouncing back to twenty. We were going along fine until another article ran and some short sellers hit our stock. We usually traded four to five thousand shares a day, but now we were trading as many as eight hundred thousand, thanks to the bad press. Short sellers could sell stock they didn't own at twenty dollars, later buying it for twelve dollars. Returning the stock they had borrowed for a profit of eight dollars per share, the short sellers made millions. The partners in the law firm that orchestrated this eventually went to prison for crimes such as this.

We believe that the scam started when the class-action attorneys produced a lead complainant who bought the stock at twenty dollars and sued on his behalf. Curiously, he was related to one of the lawyers. The complainant shareholder, who was from a little town in New Mexico, had bought two shares of stock and claimed he was hurt because of his loss. The attorneys ran ads, looking for other people to join the lawsuit and found a handful of people. And suddenly Mannatech was hit with a class-action lawsuit for a hundred million dollars. This was enormous. The lawsuit claimed we had overstated our earnings, saying that the revenue we reported would not have occurred had our salespeople not exaggerated the benefits of the product.

Our insurance company examined the case, looked at what we were being sued for, and said, "This is impossible. You reported correctly; your auditors verified it. We're not going to settle with them. They're just scam artists. This is a spurious lawsuit. There's no grounds for it. We're not going to settle." The board was concerned because the lawyers and the insurance company played a bit of ping-pong, going back and forth about settlement. The attorneys lowered their demand to ten million dollars, but the insurance company refused to settle.

"Three million is our lowest offer."

"No."

"We won't go any lower, but we'll tell you this—you'll rue the day you didn't take this offer."

When being sued for a hundred million dollars, three million seems like a bargain. The insurance company had actually offered to settle for a million, but the attorneys refused to settle for less than three million. Although we agreed to settle, we had really upset the class-action lawyers. Just as we were feeling relieved that the class action suits were over, the *Fort Worth Star Telegram* started running articles about Mannatech, accusing our distributors of saying that our products would cure cancer and other diseases. Although the company stated clearly that our products would not cure, the distributors told stories about customers becoming healthier. I didn't think the articles could get any worse, but then, on July 3, 2006, the headline read, "When is Abbott, the attorney general, going to do something about Mannatech?" We had heard that someone dumped several boxes of the plaintiff lawyer's files about our case at his office. As a result, Akin Gump had their firm in Austin meet with the attorney general staff to assure them we were anxious to comply with any issues that concerned them.

In spite of the staff's assurances, the big hit came when Greg Abbott, then Texas's attorney general, served us a cease-and-desist letter the following Monday, accusing us of saying that our products could treat, cure, or mitigate disease. He threatened to lock our doors and "throw away the key," so to speak. Having just settled one lawsuit, we'd started breathing easily and were being threatened with being put out of business if we didn't do what he said. Re-entering out of retirement was proving to be quite the rollercoaster ride.

Luckily, we had a strong law firm headed by Ken Menges of Akin Gump and good SEC lawyers. The attorney general had accused us of claiming that our product could cure cancer and other diseases, but we were very clear in all of our literature that our product did not cure cancer or any disease, although distributors had shared their belief in its ability to enhance the immune system and improve people's quality of life. They related lots of testimonials where customers told of how Mannatech products had improved their quality of life.

We began meeting with the attorney general and stopped any action while we dealt with the case. It would take us over a year to get through the lawsuit to the point of settlement. We were not charged with breaking any law, but we settled for seven million dollars, two million of which went to pay the attorney general's legal fees for putting the lawsuit together, one million fined to the CEO, and four million of which we put in a restitution fund for anyone who wanted to return the products and get their money back.

I credit this advantageous settlement to a great board of directors. As chairman of the governance committee, Jerry Gilbert, led the fight on behalf of the company. He formed a committee that included Alan Kennedy and Larry Jobe. This committee represented the company in a derivative lawsuit that followed the class-action lawsuit. It was also settled with the company agreeing to some reasonable changes.

Jerry Gilbert

"I've been general counsel to several boards, and there was no member on any of the boards like Stan. He came prepared, and as a result, I knew I had to be prepared.

He challenges people in a good way. If you're going to work with Stan, you'd better prepare. I was flattered to be asked to serve on his board because all of the time I represented the industry as a general counsel, Stan would challenge me. He made me a better lawyer. He made me prepare for every board meeting because I knew he'd be asking me some questions.

Stan is a very talented executive. He's a taskmaster and a hardworking guy. I don't think there's anyone in direct selling who had the same experience, starting from the bottom and advancing all the way to the top. I don't think there's anyone who is as experienced at every level."

As part of the settlement with the attorney general, we signed a statement stipulating that we hadn't done anything wrong and hadn't broken any laws. We had done nothing illegal, but we agreed, on pain of being "shut down," that we could not say that our product could treat, cure, or mitigate any disease and had to police our salesforce to make sure they didn't. This made it harder to speak about the advantages of the product. We couldn't tell Judy's story or any of the other hundreds of thousands of success stories about how the product had enhanced people's immune system, improving their quality of life.

As part of the settlement, the chairman and CEO had to resign and couldn't be involved in the business for five years. The board asked me to become the chairman, and when I did, everything I'd done in life seemed to have prepared me for just this role. The business had stabilized somewhat, but it had been hit hard and had gone down considerably. It has had a tough time rebounding; it's an expensive product and although we once could tell people how great the product was, the attorney general said he'd "lock the door" if he heard one word that even mentioned disease. They wouldn't even have to go to court to shut us down. To protect the company and our associates, we beefed up our compliance department and purchased software that would allow us to find any mention of disease on our associates' websites.

To help us through this crisis, we went outside and brought in a professional turnaround expert as CEO. Turns out, direct selling is enough different from typical businesses that the downturn and loss accelerated, resulted in his resignation. We then turned to a brilliant young scientist, Robert Sinnott, who was chief science officer, to take over as CEO. It seemed impossible to stop the decline, although it did slow down and the bleeding stopped. In spite of doing a good job for us, Rob decided to return to his first love and become chief science officer for another company.

We were fortunate that in spite of this chaos, we had, and have maintained, a Board of Directors to guide us through those difficult times that now includes Independent Directors. Bob Toth, former President of Avon, Larry Jobe, CPA and entrepenuer, Tyler Rameson, investor, and Eric Schrier, former president and CEO of Readers Digest. They brought in a high-powered and experienced sales executive to join us in 2007. Al Bala was the fiancé of one of our up-and-coming presidential distributors, Johanna Gil, who had witnessed the power of our products. His native language was Portuguese, but he was fluent in six languages and conversant in eleven. He held twenty-eight years of experience in opening and managing distributors in sixty countries around the world. Starting as vice president of sales, he rose through the organization and was named president and CEO in 2015. Under his leadership, Mannatech returned to revenue growth and profitability, made two critical hires in Korea and Hong Kong, slashed operating costs, and made strategic promotions and cuts at the C-level. With Al's leadership, the company is on its way back.

Al Bala, Mannatech CEO

"The greatest promise of direct sales has been that you can take care of your children and your children's children. Stan is the poster child of the promise of this industry. He represents that sense of legacy. He defied all the odds and fulfilled the industry's promise, showing how you can literally start from nothing and build multi-generational wealth.

One of the things I learned from Stan outside of the work environment came from watching him and how he handles his family. He has a sense of priorities of family first. We could be in the middle of a meeting and if one of the kids called, he'd take the call. As someone who has lived a very focused life in business, especially involving direct sales, that was very impressive to me. It's so easy to get caught up in all of the things that you do because you feel like you're helping people. Sometimes, we go overboard and don't take care of those who are the closest to us. His approach taught me how to prioritize things properly and maintain a work–life balance."

Mannatech's current leaders:
Al Bala, CEO with Landen Fredrick, CSMO

CHAPTER 7

A LEGACY OF COURAGE, CHARACTER, AND CULTURE

"The final test of a leader is that he leaves behind him in other men the conviction and the will to carry on."
Walter Lippmann

Lesson: Happiness Is Not Something You Look for–It's Found while Looking for Something

When the kids were growing up, I'd always promised them that we'd stay in the same house so they'd always be able to come home. My parents had moved around a lot while I was a kid, so I never had that yearning to go home. I wanted them to have the feeling of coming home. Later, they kidded me that we might be at the same address but that we'd remodeled the place so many times that it wasn't quite the house we'd raised them in.

Maybe their comment speaks to my love of family and warmth of home. One evening, Judy and I were on our way to Ray Robbins' house, co-founder of Mannatech, when we drove by a gated community with a sign out front reading "Italian Villa for Sale."

"Honey," I said, "We have some time before we're supposed to be there. Let's go in and take a look."

We'd been living in a homey, beautiful cottage with a great backyard for thirty-eight years, but European things had always enamored us. We liked the outside of the place, but after walking inside, we were blown away. The inside was "to die for," with a thirty-seven-foot-tall rotunda with a circular staircase that I could already see our granddaughters walking down to get married. It was ideal, and after we toured the home, Judy said, "Boy, I love this house."

"Well," I said, "I checked the price, and it's way beyond what we'd be willing to pay."

We tried to ignore the idea of the house, but she kept talking about it, and so did I. Judy had always been happy with life's simple pleasures, but I wanted to give her the home of her dreams. So I went to the guy and said, "You know, you're way out of our league, but this house has been sitting here a while. I could take it off your hands and pay you cash for it. You wouldn't have to worry."

It was a lot of money, but we ended up making a deal that we felt like we could live with. I placed a plaque on the front of the house naming it MannaVilla and dedicated it to the company's associates, who are the secret to the company's success and to our being able to enjoy that magnificent home. After getting settled into the home, I gazed into the two-acre grounds at the little hillside, a small hill that went up about ten or fifteen feet. The original landscaping was pretty bare, with only two trees. While configuring a new layout, I thought, *Ooh, that hillside back there would make a great place for a vineyard.* All it needed were some vines and trellises. What Italian villa wouldn't be enhanced by a vineyard?

My interest in grapes expanded and built momentum. I went down to Delaney Vineyard in Grapevine and talked to the people there about grapes, grape growing, and installing an irrigation system. I learned about the processes and the intricacies of being a grape grower. Since the ostrich business had trickled to a close, I also started entertaining the idea of going into the wine business at the ranch and brought it up with John. He wasn't excited about the idea, and he didn't drink much wine himself, but said with tongue in cheek that since Jesus made wine, maybe it would be okay if we did.

A vineyard consultant came up to the ranch, looking the place over for a vineyard site. He took soil samples from four or five different places and found that the sample with the best soil came from near the ostrich building and ostrich pens. That building was transformed and now operates as the tasting room for Blue Ostrich Winery & Vineyard. We made my eldest daughter, Julie, a partner. She and her husband, Pat, built and run the winery and vineyard. John Jr., my brother's son, was the partner in charge of the vineyard until he passed away in 2014. I call Julie the doyenne of wine tasting rooms because she is the best in class. She serves the best wines in the warmest and friendliest atmosphere, with the most charming smile that captivates her customers.

After the first organizational meeting in 2010, we began planting grapes in 2011, and we had our grand opening in September. It's become such a beautiful and iconic winery that it's hard to believe you're still in Texas. And it's not just pretty scenery—the grapes we grow produce wonderful-tasting wines. Enhanced by the art and skill of our winemaker Pat Whitehead, Julie's husband, who has won more than sixty medals, our 2017 Viognier is the one of which he is most proud. At the San Francisco International Wine Competition, that wine was voted a double gold, a gold medal in its class, and won best of class for all the gold medals. While I am proud of his wines, I'm also proud of his leadership in the Texas wine industry, having been elected president of the Texas Grape Growers Association.

Stan and the winemaker, Pat Whitehead, plant the first Tempranillo root stock at Blue Ostrich Vineyard

Entrance to Blue Ostrich Winery off FM 2382 Saint Jo, Tx

*Stan and daughter Julie Whitehead, managing
partner, celebrating a successful harvest.*

Philosophy: Success Is Where Preparation Meets Opportunity

Before we embarked on our wine venture, a little winery in California came
out with a white zinfandel that changed the entire view of wine in America.
All of a sudden, there was a wine that women loved to drink. Everybody
began talking about wine, and popularity increased so much that people
were buying it by the case instead of the bottle. In an online *Forbes* article,
Bob Trinchero, winemaker at Sutter Home, Napa Valley, said, "I am struck
by how many people tell me, 'I hate to admit it, but my entry to wine was
white zinfandel.'" Unknown to us at the time, it was events such as this and
the 1976 World's Fair, when a Napa Valley winery won first prize against
the great French wines, that gave us a great opportunity.

Around the same time as the first Blue Ostrich organizational meeting,
we bought a business called Wine Shop At Home, although we originally
invested in the company back in 2005, right after I harvested my first crop
of grapes from the backyard vineyard. No doubt that was what piqued my
interest in the wine business.

A lot of good things in my life originated with the Direct Selling Association. Another of them was meeting a guy named John Lynch. During the dot.com craze, a lot of wine companies had formed and then discovered they couldn't sell wine on the web. Warehouses were full of wine that people couldn't sell, so Lynch capitalized on that and formed a company called 1800-WINESHOP, raised a lot of money, and bought a bunch of that wine. He built a website, got a phone number, and started selling it through telephone sales.

After experiencing a bit of difficulty with sales, he ran ads for a wine-tasting at a hotel's banquet room. Hundreds of people came to taste the wine. The event must have really been something because one of the people attending soon asked, "Would you come over and do this same thing for some friends at my house?" A trend started of people asking for home wine tastings, which eventually raised enough curiosity for some of them to inquire about being a sales consultant themselves.

During our initial meeting, Lynch said, "Things are going really well. I'm taking on some shareholders. You ought to become a shareholder and join me."

He was selling stock for two dollars a share, trying to raise several million dollars.

"Sounds a little risky for me," I said, "Tell you what, I'll lend you three hundred thousand dollars at 6 percent interest if you give me an option at two dollars per share for 150,000 shares so long as I can exercise it at any time. You'll have the money, and yet I'll always have the option to be a shareholder."

"Okay," he said. "It's a deal."

Afterward, I began following the business more closely. It continued to grow, but the momentum slowed and so did the growth. He came to me and admitted he needed a substantial investment. I didn't buy the stock, but I did offer to lend more money since he'd been good about paying his interest. Not too long after that, when the interest payments slowed, I looked at his books closely and discovered he wasn't making any money. I wasn't surprised when the next time we met he asked me to buy the business outright. To protect the money I'd already lent him, we wrote a new note with protection, and I offered to lend the company money at 8 percent interest with an option to convert the note at my option to 75 percent of Wine Shop At Home.

He agreed, which took his and the other shareholders' combined ownership from 100 percent to 25 percent. Yet, they reasoned that was better
than losing everything. The loan required that they turn over control of
the company to us immediately. I asked my son, Stan II, who I was very
proud of as a proven producer and leader, to lead the company as chairman

Stan II and Jane relax with directors' school
participants at the Fredrick Ranch

of the board. Having worked together for over thirty years, I had watched
him grow from sales to operations to president of a very successful launch
in Canada. Jane Edwards Creed, one of the brilliant marketing executives
who had helped a top party-plan business go from two hundred million
dollars to almost a billion dollars in sales, had been recently elected CEO
and was asked to remain.

Under Stan II's leadership, he turned the ship around, cut expenses, and reduced salaries. He brought Marlene Cain, who had helped Cameo become successful, on board to convert their home wine-tasting model to the hostess-driven party-plan model. Stan II, Jane, and Marlene, working with the two senior executive directors, Diane Nozik and Tammy Nichols, soon had consultants booking shows, hostess coaching, recruiting, building, and developing their businesses.

Within that first year, the company became profitable, and since then it has grown at about 15 to 20 percent per year. After two years, we converted our notes and now own an exciting, innovative direct-selling business.

Lesson: Success Is Never Final–Failure Is Never Fatal

Over the years, the health of our businesses made remarkable strides but our personal health hit temporary setbacks.

In January of 2017, we had just gotten settled in Maui at our condo for our winter vacation when I was notified that my brother John had another setback and was not expected to live. We rushed back home and went directly to the hospital. John was in and out of consciousness yet seemed to recognize my voice. I assured him that he could go to home in the sky where he could speak again, knowing not being able to talk really frustrated him. I silently pledged I would take care of everything to arrange our estates as we had planned. He passed away quietly the next day. It was almost as if he was waiting on me to get there.

John and I had met at 7 a.m. in Muenster every Friday morning at Rohmer's café for years. Over breakfast, we discussed our family partnerships and the ranch. Since John had lost his ability to talk a year prior, we had not been meeting. For some reason, I felt the need to call him to have breakfast just one more time. We ate in silence, and then we went out to the ranch, drove the land, inspected the cattle, and walked the vineyard before sitting in the swing on the front porch to enjoy the sounds of the cattle mooing, the birds singing, and the flags flapping in the breeze. John seemed to sense some finality in that meeting, and I, too, was concerned this could be the last one. Two weeks later, he experienced a severe setback and never saw the ranch again.

We buried Mom the following July of 2017. Almost ninety-nine years old, losing John seemed to be too much for her. I consoled myself knowing they both lived long and productive lives, knowing the world was better off because they were here and would never be the same with them gone.

In January of 2021, we took the final steps in dissolving John and my partnerships. In keeping with John's wishes, I bought the ranch and the winery from his family, leaving them the acreage John loved so much. Now, the Fredrick ranch could pass on to the next generation.

In January 2018, I opted for my second hip replacement. Rehab seemed to be going well until two weeks after the operation, when it started to get sore; on the evening of February 13, it erupted. Fluids started spewing out of the weep hole. During the ambulance ride to the hospital, I still didn't think anything about the situation being critical. The doctors tested it and realized it was sepsis—they couldn't kill the infection. My health went downhill for several days. Unknown to me at the time, the doctor had told Judy and the children, "People don't survive sepsis. Don't get your hopes up."

My family did not believe it, even though they knew the prognosis, and I never felt terminal. The doctor hadn't shared that information with me. I didn't see myself as being terminally ill. Maybe that line of thinking can be traced back to my experience with Mom and the bumblebee, tying into the power of the mind. As Frankl said, "If the why is strong enough, the how will come." Death never entered my mind as an option—I didn't feel the pain or recognize the possibility, although the kids did tell me later that I had been delirious and wasn't talking too clearly.

The major infection cleared in a month or two, but while searching for the source of the infection, they discovered colon cancer and removed about a foot of colon. They told me that they'd got it all, but the hip couldn't be replaced until all chances of infection were gone. So they inserted a temporary mechanism that allowed me to touch my toe down and move around a little. I couldn't place any weight on it, but somehow in therapy, it knocked loose and had to be removed, which forced me to be in a wheelchair until I'd healed enough for surgery.

My body finally fought through the infection, and in November of that year, they replaced my hip. Having spent over nine months in the hospital or a rehab center that year, I immediately planned a trip to Hawaii for Christmas to celebrate being able to walk. I invited the entire family, kids, grandkids, everyone—all thirty-one of us.

The entire Fredrick family, except for Brandon who was serving in the Marines.

Part of the health maintenance for cancer is a CT scan of the area every six months. In 2020, the doctors came to me and said, "Oh, wait a minute—you've got a problem."

"It's nothing. I feel great, so it couldn't be anything," I said.

"Well, the scan found a mass on the spine. We're going to check and send you in for a biopsy."

They found it was high-grade B-cell lymphoma, so I went through chemotherapy and then radiation. The last time they checked, there wasn't any activity at all. Now in the clear and feeling great, the only indication of my ordeal is the surgeon told me to walk with a cane to ensure I did not fall. Other than that, my mind has carried me back into a normal state of being. So, I hope Churchill was right, and the cane makes me look more distinguished.

Through all my time at the hospital, Judy never left my side. This precious woman stayed by my side, rarely ever leaving, sleeping on a rollaway in the room, for most of the year. We were elated when I finally had a clear health report. I felt good, and she felt good. Then, all of a sudden, she couldn't take deep breaths; the doctors diagnosed her with chronic lymphatic leukemia. She couldn't breathe well, so the doctor drained the fluid on her lungs. Even so, she had a real tough time for a year. After chemo treatments, all signs of the lymphoma are gone.

We're both healthy and ready for the next decade. Next stop—a hundred! We'll admit to having had some bumps in the road along the way, but we never, ever give up.

Judy, wife

I have an intuitiveness. When it happened, I knew one thing was that I wouldn't leave him. No one in the hospital ever asked me to leave or to stay away. I was constantly with him because I felt it was really necessary, not only for me, but he was in pretty bad shape. It was one of those times when the doctors didn't think he could pull through. All our children gathered around in the waiting room and wouldn't leave.

The infection had started on his brain, and he wasn't talking very rational about anything. For the first couple of weeks, we didn't know what was going to happen to him, but they had good medicines, and one of them actually worked on the infection. With his mind cleared, he was calm, grateful, and became the one to reassure us: *No worries; everything is okay.*

Patrick, son-in-law

"It is a rare occasion when Stan gives any outward indication of vulnerability and struggle. He is a big believer in the fact that it's not what happens to you but rather how you react to things that matters.

During his long and difficult health comeback, I remember being with him in Dallas the spring of 2018 at one of the *many* rehab facilities he was in during much of that year. As I was helping Judy move him from a hospital bed into a wheelchair, he looked at me with a weary face and with a big sigh and said, 'Pat, I just can't figure out how I got here.'

He didn't mean it in the sense that he didn't know how he got to that facility. It was more the overarching question 'How did I end up in this whole situation?' But at the end of that conversation, he said, 'Well, I've just got to keep doing what the doctors and everyone else keep telling me I have to do so we can go sailing again.'

He just kept pushing himself and refused to give up . . . in a situation where someone with less fortitude would throw in the towel in a second. He draws strength from Judy and from the entire family, and he felt like there was so much work left to do he just had to get through the thing."

Philosophy: Compassion Influences, and You Can Say a Lot without Saying Anything at All

In between the hip replacement surgeries, I traveled with Landen, my second son, who I am so proud of, and who works with Mannatech as chief sales and marketing officer, to South Africa for a business trip. After graduating from ACU and then going on to get his MBA, Landen started with the company as a consultant on internet protocols and proved invaluable to the sales department. Brought on as a VP of sales, he has moved up ever since and was recently elected as chief sales and marketing officer. In addition, he is chairman of the board of the M5M Foundation.

Cape Town is one of the most beautiful cities I've seen, very picturesque. Yet, behind this beautiful landscape are thousands of children suffering from malnutrition and even starvation. We became aware of this when we found that Louis and Leone Van Der Linde were using Mannatech products to provide nutrition to an orphanage and saw amazing results with the children's health, attendance, and grades. Other children's homes heard about the results and asked for the products. This inspired Louis and Leone to also provide the products to the citizens of South Africa. Consequently, with their help, Mannatech opened South Africa where the business has grown steadily ever since, and they are now platinum presidential associates.

The health of the children in these orphanages improved so dramatically that the representatives of Kids Around the World asked us to partner and provide nutrition with their meals. Landen and the M5M executive director Sara Louthan worked with Kids Around the World, forging a partnership that provided twenty million meals in 2019. While we were in South Africa, I was fortunate enough to witness the incredible difference our products make in these kids. After a few business meetings, we visited some of the orphanages that the foundation sponsors in rural villages outside Cape Town—typically a house with its rooms converted into dormitories. The kids were lively and talked enthusiastically as the director told us their stories:

> "When she came here, her growth was stunted. She wasn't able to learn because she was so sick."

> "The reason we like you so much is because after we started giving the fortified nutritional food, kids began to grow again."

> "He can learn now and does not get sick as often."

The manager of the orphanage guided us into the gymnasium, and just as some fine waltz music began to play, he said, "Let me show you what these kids can do."

Two kids, who looked like they were maybe in the third or fourth grade, waltzed across the floor to the music, like something that you'd see in a fine theater performance. The way they glided across the floor was so beautiful that I thought, *Wow, if what we're doing can help kids get to where they can do that, then we have really done something significant.* Not only were the kids smart enough to perform the steps, but they were also physically fit enough to do them.

Being in South Africa was exhilarating—to be and see where Nelson Mandela had inspired people and ended apartheid. During his twenty-five years of imprisonment, Mandela regularly recited the same poem with a gentle spirit and a strong voice: *Invictus* by William Ernest Henley. Here are two of my favorite verses.

> "Out of the night that covers me,
> Black as the pit from pole to pole,
> I thank whatever Gods may be
> For my unconquerable soul . . . .
> It matters not how strait the gate,
> How charged with punishments the scroll,
> I am the master of my fate,
> I am the captain of my soul."

It's good to remind ourselves that Mandela was able to influence people because he didn't lose that indomitable spirit, no matter his circumstances. He never gave up.

Landen, second son and fifth child

"When Dad and I had an opportunity to go to South Africa for business, he started doing a really peculiar thing. On a photo safari, it took so much to get him to look at the camera. All he wanted to do when we took pictures was to have the picture show him looking up at me. Dad believed in recognition, and he consistently recognized others to help them believe what he saw possible."

Philosophy: What We Do in Life Echoes in Eternity

In the movie *Gladiator*, Russell Crowe, portraying the Roman general Maximus, addresses his terrified troops before battle: "In two months, I will be at my villa, harvesting my crops. Where will you be? *Imagine it and it will be so*...Brothers, what we do in life...echoes in eternity."

After Dad died, Mom gave me a pair of leather shoes that he'd worn as a two- or three-year-old little boy. They sit on the ledge of the fireplace in my library, where I pass them nearly every day as I go to my desk. They are a constant reminder that I have big shoes to fill if I am to live up to his legacy—not a legacy of prosperity or wealth but instead a legacy of courage, character, culture, and family.

Benjamin Disraeli once said, "The greatest good you can do for another is not just share your riches but to reveal to him his own."

★★★

John and Dorothy, parents of Stan and John Fredrick

CHAPTER 8

STAY CALM DURING STORMS

*"My interest is in the future because I am going
to spend the rest of my life there."*
Charles Kettering

Philosophy: Don't Force It–Be Patient–Take Your Time

Dad was the kind of guy who could do anything, someone you'd like
to have around under any circumstances. Because he approached life so
calmly, there was no crisis that couldn't be handled. Whether fixing a car
or putting a bike together, he always said, "Don't force it. Be patient. Take
your time."

When I was in the fifth or sixth grade, while Dad was teaching me
how to fix my bicycle, he hit his finger and cut it open. Blood gushed
everywhere, but he didn't explode or even react except to say "Ouch,"
then wrap it up and go on about his work.

"Didn't that hurt, Dad?" I asked.

"Of course," he said.

"Why didn't you cry or scream or something?"

"Well," he said, "it doesn't hurt any less if I scream or cry."

From that I learned you can experience pain but choose not to increase the suffering. You can choose where to place the attention and energy. This helped me flow with life more, no matter the weather or circumstance.

Another Sunday morning, Dad took me to ride my bike. We came to a fork on a gravel road, and when he changed directions, the bike slipped out from under him. He put his arm down to catch himself and threw his shoulder out of socket. When he stood up, his arm just dangled. It looked like the kind of thing that would make an ordinary person scream out in pain. On the walk back to the house, in a calm and matter-of-fact way, he said, "We'll see if we can get a doctor to put this back in place."

You can choose where to place the attention and energy.

The doctor later took Dad's arm in his hands and shoved it back in the socket. Dad winced a little, but there was no screaming or hollering. For some people, that would have been a major event, but for him it was just another day. Dad had the ability to remain calm during a storm. If something hit him or hurt him, he just got up and kept going. Watching his demeanor throughout my life made me want to be the same way. Over the years, this desire helped me choose how to respond in various situations instead of with a knee-jerk reaction. Reacting takes away from the time we have to think clearly or act on the moment, and this ability certainly came in handy during my first sailing adventure.

Philosophy: Stay Calm during Storms

Throughout my life, my interest and dream for sailing never diminished. In 2007, I finally reached the point at which I was ready take on a big ocean adventure. My son, Stan, and I had read about a deal where we could buy an interest in a sailboat docked at Lake Texoma, about an hour from the Dallas metroplex. In preparation for renting the boat, we enrolled in sailing lessons on a thirty-six-foot Hunter until we knew what to do and how to do it well enough to earn our American Sailing Association (ASA) certification.

We loved gliding across the water, but Lake Texoma was a small lake, and we could hardly wait to get to the ocean and sail a bigger boat. After contacting a charter company in the British Virgin Islands and making arrangements to take out a fifty-four-foot Juneau, Stan, Landen, and I, with Patrick and Robert, two of my sons-in-law, set out with Les, our original instructor, as our captain.

Sailing across the Sir Francis Drake Channel to the Indian Islands, we learned how to tie up to a buoy and take a dinghy over to the dock. The next day, we sailed down the island and around Tortola. We docked at Jost Van Dyke for the night, and the next day we sailed across the channel and docked at Cane Garden Bay for the night.

The next morning, our group sailed toward The Bitter End, a harbor at the end of Virgin Gorda—the last place before you'd hit the big blue waters that leads to Africa. While on the water, we'd seen squalls pop up on the horizon in the distance, but while in open water between Tortola and Virgin Gorda, the water started to get a little choppier and the wind came up a little stronger. The question became what we should do when we hit a squall. Stan and I looked at each other, looked at Captain Les, and asked, "Should we lower the sails?"

Les took a moment to look at the raging water Mother Nature had produced and said, "Naaaah. It'll be fine."

Looking back at whitecaps across the water again, a question spread across his face as my son, Stan, asked, "Should we reef the sail? Maybe bring it down just a little bit?"

"No," he said.

Soon the sky turned black and rain poured. We had no idea whether it was a squall or an outright storm. The wind whipped the rain around the boat and cut visibility. Our captain was more used to calm lake waters than turbulent ocean waters and didn't know what to do. Stan was at the helm on one side of the boat, keeping us into the wind, and I stood the helm on the other. But all I could do was keep a lookout, hoping to keep us from running ashore or into another boat. I was stunned at how far the boat heeled to its side. Theoretically, a boat that big won't tip over, but the wind blew so hard, it seemed as if that could happen at any moment. Realizing someone might be thrown overboard, I told everyone to put on lifejackets.

Pat, son-in-law

Even in adverse times in his life, I've never seen Stan shaken. He's always very composed, and this storm moment was certainly a situation that would have challenged anybody's composure. The boat started moving pretty good, and I had one those feelings where you think *This is not how I thought it would be.* The storm lasted thirty or forty minutes, but it seemed like forever.

We're thoughtful about our safety on the boat, but typically we're not wearing life jackets. When he started passing out life jackets, I think I was aware that he was concerned about our safety, as he had four young men on that boat who were under his charge. With whatever decisions he had made or that we were going to make together, his number-one priority was to get through safely. He sprang into action with the undercurrent of *Let's be safe about this, and let's be smart.*

For thirty minutes we went through harrowing, white, knuckle-biting fear. For first-time sailors, this was our baptism of fire. Some people get a big rush from that type of fear, but I'm not one of them. I don't search for those kinds of thrills. But in the moment, while busy taking action, you don't have time to be scared, let alone paralyzed by fear.

When I'm watching someone, I have more fear than when I'm doing something myself. When I do it, I'm in control. When I watch, it's easier for fear to creep in. When I find myself in the thick of it, I find the courage to face it and not let it beat me. And although we were scared to death, we ended up sailing through that storm. I enjoyed the rush after it was over, but I wouldn't search for it. I will combat the fear, but I won't seek it.

Stan II, first son

When in the squall, the sixty-foot mast was swaying back and forth, and the boom was crashing across the deck like crazy, threatening to tear the boat apart and capsizing it in the process. At least, that's the way we all felt. Dad remained calm throughout, and he and I began working the lines. Between seeing the calm on his face and the act of 'staying busy,' it kept me calm as well. It's not that I wasn't scared because I definitely was; it was that I had no time to be frozen by the fear because of the actions we were taking.

I know he was scared, too, but he never showed it. That's always been his way, always to be that calm presence, and it doesn't even seem hard for him. Just natural. Afterward, he admitted that he was worried, but in the moment he did whatever he could to calm us.

After riding through the storm, opting for a dry night's sleep and a warm meal, we docked at Spanish Town and waited for the weather to clear. Our shaking legs happily standing on dry land, we joked that now we knew why the place we were headed was called The Bitter End. The first big storm in the blue water shook us, but just as in life generally, once we made it to the "The Bitter End" port, that experience actually ended up being one of our most memorable trips. Sailing was better than anything I could have imagined. Whether standing on the bow of the boat with the salt spray in my face or at the helm facing a strong wind, with the boat heeling so much I could drag my hand in the water, it was the most exhilarating experience I could ever imagine.

That first adventure gave me a passion for sailing, and I went back every year for five years until my hip replacement. After life's choppy health storms, the boys and I decided it is finally time to return to the waters, and we've made plans to set sail in December 2021.

Landen, second son and fifth child

Dad sees things in a logical sequence. Standing with his face in the wind, everything can be swirling around him, but he remains calm.

While the boat almost capsized, Dad calmly worked the ropes. He even looked over and gave me a gentle smile as if to say Isn't this fun? Everything is going to be okay.

These pictures demonstrate two of my big dreams:
sailing a sloop in the Caribbean and elk hunting
on horseback in the mountains of Colorado

★★★

Philosophy: Think for the Long Term—Build for the Bigger Vision

When I received the Lifetime Achievement Award in 2019, I still felt like more needed to be done, and a lot of that was ensuring that our family legacy would be perpetual. They say your legacy is what is left after you're gone, and I've been working on that since.

In spring 2021, *Direct Selling News* nominated me, along with five others who had worked fifty years or more in the industry, as an inaugural Legends Honoree. The interview series, together with reuniting with men who I'd worked with in the past, spurred thoughts of leaving a legacy behind and deciding my vision for the future. I did not realize at the time that we would soon be in the middle of a world-wide pandemic that would shake the very foundation of our person-to-person, party-plan, and tasting-room businesses. Our legacy was already at risk.

The family decided that we would meet on a Zoom call every Sunday afternoon. The meeting would give us a chance to see how our families and our businesses were handling the pandemic. As of September of 2021, we are still meeting, gaining strength, getting information, and sharing solutions.

The Covid-19 virus could not have been more disruptive to our businesses if it had been designed to attack it. The national mandates that occurred had a direct impact on the way we do business. Wine Shop At Home was built around home wine tastings with four or five couples. With restrictions on the size of meetings, social distancing, and wearing of masks, it became almost impossible, if not illegal, to get people together.

To counter this, Stan II and Jane helped the team create a virtual tasting scenario. It involved sending the guest list provided by the hostess three bottles of wine. Two of which they purchased for the going price, but the third they purchased for only $9.95. At the set time, everyone signed into the event as instructed by the consultant. They were then able to hear and see the consultant explain the wines as they tasted them. Miraculously, the party sales increased as well as sales by active consultants. This allowed our consultants to continue earning money and stay in business.

Blue Ostrich Winery had a bigger problem because all restaurants, bars, and wineries were closed for about four months between April and August. They were only able to open if they could be classified as a restaurant. This meant over half of the sales had to be non-alcoholic. Julie and Patrick put together a plan that included adding all-day lunch to the menu, promote souvenir sales, and enhance the sale of charcuterie boards to go with the tastings.

To handle social distancing and a mandate to serve no more than fifty percent of capacity at a time, they instituted a reservation system, serving four time slots a day on Thursday, Friday, Saturday, and Sunday. This allowed a maximum of fifty customers at each seating. The response was overwhelming, resulting in an increase in sales for the year in spite of being closed for four months.

Custom Fit Bra Company consultants were unable to create new customers because the bra is fitted on the customer. My daughter Jamie encouraged them to use this time to service their existing customers by email, text, phone, and FaceTime. CFBC kept their consultants in business as they focused on existing customers.

Ashly's consulting business, BioBalance, emphasizing mind, heart, and body balance, was also based on person-to-person contact. When Covid-19 hit, she adjusted and immediately began switching to online sessions. As a result, she was able to see more people and increase her revenue.

At Mannatech, Al and Landen also had to pivot. They found new ways to stay in touch with major associates and country managers. Instead of having four executives travel the world, seeing people only once or twice a year, they switched to Zoom calls at least once a week for each country. This increased the personal contact as they were able to discuss best ways to serve nutritional supplements to a very health-conscious world. The company was also able to increase sales during the pandemic.

This could have been a disaster, and possibly end or at least setback our legacy companies. Yet management teams rose to the occasion and responded with our family's *never ever give up* culture.

★★★

The direct sales industry gave me the opportunity to create generational wealth, to build a legacy, to take care of my children and my children's children. I worked my entire life within the industry to build the Fredrick legacy, and luckily, I have my children to carry it into the future. I don't have it all figured out, but part of my dream includes passing the torch to them.

As for me, my dreams continue to unfold as life moves forward, ever in pursuit of a bigger vision. Things keep happening in life, and while I continue to build the businesses and the Fredrick legacy, I know part of perseverance is falling in love with life's impermanence and having a willingness to evolve as time progresses, recognizing some endings are just another beginning. Behind every ending lies the start of a new chapter, a new beginning.

Blue Ostrich
WINERY / VINEYARD

5611 FM2382, St Jo, TX 76265

Contact Us: (940) 995.3100
Thursday - Saturday 12p - 6p |
Sunday 12p - 5p

Welcome to the family owned and operated Blue Ostrich Winery & Vineyard. For many years this facility was one of the foremost ostrich breeding and ranching facilities in the southwest. The structure that houses our winery, tasting room and corporate offices was once filled with ostrich eggs, chicks and fledglings. The acreage to the west that nurtures our Tempranillo, Viognier and Cabernet grapevines was the same hillside where hundreds of 7 foot tall ostrich roamed during the 80's and 90's.

As our ostrich ranching adventure drew to a close and we relinquished our herd, the future of the seven birds remaining was uncertain . . . until we needed a name for our winery and vineyard. Today our feathered friends not only adorn the Blue Ostrich label, they also function as as our official winery mascots and welcome you to our beautiful Red River Valley.

STAN'S FAVORITE QUOTES AND SPEECHES

Quotes

"The greatest use of a life is to spend it on something that will outlast it."
—William James

"The future belongs to those who believe in their dreams."
—Franklin Delano Roosevelt

"People seldom improve when they have no model but themselves to copy after."
—Oliver Goldsmith

"Every action in our lives touches on some chord that will vibrate in eternity."
—Edwin Hubbel Chapin

"Destiny is no matter of chance. It is a matter of choice. *It is* not *a thing to be waited for, it is a thing to be achieved."*
—William Jennings Bryan

"Fame is a vapor, popularity an accident, and riches take wings. Only one thing endures and that is character."
—Horace Greeley

"In the end, everything will be okay. If it's not okay, it's not yet the end."
—Fernando Sabino

"If the why is there, the how will come."
—Viktor Frankl

"Only those who will risk going too far can possibly find out how far one can go."

—T. S. Eliot

"Only those who attempt the absurd can achieve the impossible."

—Albert Einstein

"That which does not kill me makes me stronger."

—Nietzsche

"One has to pay dearly for immortality; one has to die several times while one is still alive."

—Nietzsche

"Reason and judgment are qualities of a great leader."

—Tacitus

"Some are born great, some achieve greatness, and some have greatness thrust upon them."

—Shakespeare, *Twelfth Night*

"It's easy to flatter; it's harder to praise."

—Jean Paul Richter

"The great hope of society is individual character."

—William Ellery Channing

"Events of great consequence often spring from trifling circumstances."

—Titus Livy

"*If you don't know where you are going,
you'll end up someplace else.*"

—Yogi Berra

"If you don't know *where* you *are* going,
any road will *get* you there."

—Lewis Carroll

"Blessed are the young, for they shall
inherit the national debt."

—Herbert Hoover

"*It is a* simple *procedure to* calculate *the* number
of seeds *in an* apple. But *who* among us can
ever say *how* many apples *are in a* seed?"

—Wayne W. Dyer

"*Out of mud the lovely lotus blossoms, out
of trials something higher rises.*"

—Raymond Ng

"My interest is in the future because I am
going to spend the rest of my life there."

—Charles Kettering

"*If there be any truer measure of a man than by
what he does, it must be by what he gives.*"

—Robert South

"*Glory follows virtue as if it were its shadow.*"

—Marcus Tullius Cicero

"Glory *is* fleeting, but obscurity is forever."
—Napoleon Bonaparte

"It is all very well to copy what you see, but it is better to draw what you see in your mind. Then your memory and imagination are freed from the training imposed by nature."
—Edgar Degas

"For this is what America is all about. It is the uncrossed desert and the unclimbed ridge. It is the star that is not reached and the harvest that is sleeping in the unplowed ground."
—Lyndon B. Johnson

"A thing of beauty is a joy for ever:
Its loveliness increases; it will never
Pass into nothingness."
—John Keats

"To gild refined gold, to paint the lily,
To throw a perfume on the violet,
To smooth the ice, or add another hue
Unto the rainbow, or with taper-light
To seek the beauteous eye of heaven to garnish,
Is wasteful and ridiculous excess."
—Shakespeare, *The Life and Death of King John*

"We are born *with only* one face, but laughing or crying, wisely *or* unwisely, *eventually* we *form our own.*"
—Coco Chanel

"The perfection of outward loveliness is the soul shining through its crystalline covering."
—Jane Porter

"What is beautiful is good, and who is good will soon be beautiful."
—Sappho

"Success consists of getting up just one more time than you fall."
—Oliver Goldsmith

"A friend is a gift you give yourself."
—Robert Louis Stevenson

"Laughter is the shortest distance between two people."
—Victor Borge

"Choose a job you love, and you will never have to work a day in your life."
—Confucius

"To know someone here or there with whom you can feel, there is an understanding in spite of distance or thoughts expressed—that can make of this earth a garden."
—Goethe

"There is in every woman a spark of heavenly fire."
—Washington Irving

"The mold of a person's future, the shape of her life and destiny, and the sum total of all her accomplished achievements is in her own hands that holds the invisible brush that paint pictures on the walls of her mind."
—Henry James

"The legend of the Alamo was created not because Colonel Travis sacrificed his life, but because he decided where to draw the line.
—Stan Fredrick

"This is what America is all about. It is the uncrossed desert, and the unclaimed ridge. It is the star that is not reached and the harvest that is sleeping in the unplowed grounds."
—Lyndon Johnson

"Character consists of what you do on the third and fourth tries."
—James Michener

"Unstoppable people are ignited by purpose, enabled by belief, equipped by preparation, and rewarded by perseverance."
—Unknown

"The secret of staying young is to live honestly, eat slowly, and lie about your age."
—Lucille Ball

"The difference between try and triumph is a little umph."
—Marvin Phillips

"You never will *be the person* you can *be if pressure,*
tension *and* discipline *are* taken out *of* your life."
                                    —Dr. James Bilkey

" *"A Goal Is A Dream With A Deadline"*
                                    —Napoleon Hill

*"Losing your sight is not the worst thing that
can happen—it's losing your vision."*
                                    —Helen Keller

"If you walk backwards, you **will never** stub your toe."
                                    —Harvey MacKay

"Never **doubt that a** small group **of thoughtful,
committed citizens can** change the world;
indeed, it's the only thing that ever has."
                                    —Margaret Mead

"If that doesn't light your fire, your wood is wet."
                                    —Mary Crowley

"People *don't* care *how* much you know *until* they
know *how* much you care."
                                    —Theodore Roosevelt

"If you always do *what* you always did, you
will always get *what* you always *got.*"
                                    —Albert Einstein

"She who rides a tiger finds it difficult to dismount."
                                    —Chinese Proverb

"A dream without belief is just a wish."

—Unknown

"Accept the challenges so that you can feel the exhilaration of victory."

—George S. Patton

"Happiness is not something you look for. It is found when looking for something."

—Stan Fredrick

Imagine It, Act on It, Die for It
Delivered at Mannatech Presidential Meeting

All of us hate war. No doubt about it. We all hate it. But some of the best lessons in life come from warriors because it's the warrior that actually puts his life on the line. Sometimes, we put our feelings on the line. We put our time on the line. We put things on the line, but we never do put our lives on the line. Sometimes, they come out with some of the best words of inspiration, the best symbols of leadership that you will find almost anywhere. There was a Korean warrior who was reported to have said this on his deathbed: "Do not weep. Do not notify my men of my death. Beat the drums. Blow the trumpet. Wave the flag to advance. We fight on." This message from a deathbed shows incredible perseverance, incredible courage, incredible ability to go on and on until they win.

If you go halfway around the world several centuries later, you'll find Marcus Aurelius saying some very similar words to encourage his troops. You probably saw a replica of this in the movie *Gladiator.*

If you all saw that movie, Russell Crowe played the part of Maximus, who was apparently representing Marcus Aurelius. It was a cold, frosty morning. The soldiers were scared to death because the enemy had just sent their messenger, the Roman messenger, back tied to his horse without a head, striking fear in the heart of everyone there. Maximus said to his men as he rode his steed, the nervous prancing horse in front of his soldiers, "Three weeks from now, I will be harvesting my crops. Imagine where you will be, and it will be so. Imagine where you will be, and it will be so. What we do here today will echo in eternity."

These are strong words, strong feelings, but words that we can take and help motivate us. Because while we are not facing death in its ultimate sense, as I have quoted that line from *Hope for the Flowers* before, that we don't die. *"What looks like you will die, but what is really you will still live.* Life is changed, not taken away."

As we look to the future, we must begin to think about what these lessons tell us about life and about how to conduct our business. What can we learn from these two examples? Well, to me, there are three things that I take away. The first is "imagine it." The second is "act on it." The third is "die for it." With those three philosophies, those three courses of action, we can change our lives and change the lives of everybody around us. What does it mean to imagine it? It means deciding where you want to go.

Zig Ziglar said that the greatest characters, the strongest people, are those who have a mission that they must accomplish. We must have a mission that we want to accomplish. Those missions can be the grand mission of your life, or they can be the day-to-day missions of what you have to do to get there. All I can suggest is that you make sure as you think about this mission in life that you make it measurable and attainable. Don't just say, "I'm going to have to be better tomorrow than I was today."

That's not a measurable goal. You must decide what you want to be. And isn't it wonderful that we now have a compensation plan that will help us visualize where we want to be and be able to set those goals easily? If I were you, I would look at those lists, and I would see where I am and where I want to be. I would probably have a goal for this year.

I would have a goal for this month. I would have a goal for five years, and I would make it specific. You can make those goals related to our compensation plan. You can have them related to your income level. You can have them related to how many people you're going to recruit this month, how many people you're going to talk to. You have such an opportunity to imagine it, but the beauty of to imagine it is what Maximus said in the film, "If you imagine it, it will be so."

The second thing is we must act on it. Someone once said that a good plan unacted on is not as important as a bad plan acted on. We must begin to visualize what the warrior meant when he said, "Beat the drum. Blow the trumpet. Wave the flag." What does that mean in your life? Well, for some of us, it means just get out of bed. For some of us, it means we must go on. For some of us, it means get in the car. For some of us, it means pick up the telephone. But we must take action. We must begin to move.

Because if we don't move, nothing is going to happen. Once you decide on your goal, then the very next step is the action to accomplish it. Thomas Jefferson once said, "Action defines the man." If you find yourself talking and not acting, the definition is probably not what you want it to be. If you find yourself thinking and not acting, you probably won't reach that goal. Maxwell Maltz said that we are all teleological.

By the way, his book, *Psycho-Cybernetics*, sold 30 million copies to people who wanted to improve their lives. Teleological means that we are an organism that is inherently goal oriented. It means that we will accomplish whatever we imagine and whatever we decide we want to be. But we really have to decide it. We really have to believe it. Rory Vaden, in the book called *Take The Stairs*, which I recommend to you, stated that the Law of Action means no matter what we say, our actions will show exactly what we believe.

In other words, the Law of Action says, if you believe it, your actions will reflect that belief. Stop and think about it. Every day when you wake up, are your actions reflecting that goal that you imagined? If they're not, you might want to stop and examine that one more time and decide if you're where you want to be and if you're doing what you want to do. The other thing great about action is what Norman Vincent Peale said that *the great thing about action is, is that it restores our confidence.*

It makes us believe once again. It makes us understand who we are and that we can accomplish what we believe. Again, I like what Zig Ziglar said, you don't have to be great to start, but you have to start to be great. Those who are great start. If you want to be great, then you start. Action is the secret to greatness. Confucius said, "God provides the wind. Man must raise the sails." Something for us all to remember. What we need to accomplish is provided. The good Lord has provided what we need to reach our goals. All we have to do is take action and raise the sails.

The third premise after *Imagining it* and *Acting on it* is *Dying for it,* which means simply to be willing to give up things that you want for things that you have to have, things that you would rather do for things that you need to do. As we begin to think about this goal that we have imagined, as we begin to think about the things that we need to do to get there, then we will realize that we're going to have to give up something.

You will have to give up something. Some things will not be what you want them to be all the time. You'll have to give up something. You may even have to give up watching that wonderful series that you just have to watch. I mean, *Game of Thrones* is going to happen no matter whether you're there or not. But I know a lot of people who have to be in front of that TV to watch that serial. You may have to give that up. You may have to give up that date night with your wife. You may have to give up that vacation that you were going to take. You may have to give up something. But the secret will be, if you're willing to give it up, then all of a sudden, the world opens up to you because you are willing in a sense to die for what you believe. A lot of times, we have to ask ourselves why. *Why do I want to do this? Why will I give up this much?* And all I can tell you is, as Viktor Frankl said it best in *Man's Search for Meaning:* If the why is strong enough, the how will come.

Go back and look at your mission. Is it really your mission? Is it something you really are passionate about? If it is, if that is your mission and you are passionate about it, the how will come. It will happen to you. Someone once said, you just can't beat a person who won't quit. And I think we have a room of people here who won't quit.

A modern-day American general said that his greatest desire was that his son see him as a father instead of as a warrior. He wrote a prayer. He called it "Build Me a Son, O Lord," and he wrote this prayer outlining all of the different things that it takes to be a great person, a great man in this life, and to lead a happy life. It was one of the most stirring things that I've ever read. I read it over to my children, and I have tried to practice it. But it's one of those things that you can never feel complete about, but yet it has so many aspirational qualities that each of us can do.

I think it's especially meaningful that it's written by a warrior, General Douglas MacArthur. Someone who I think even those of you from other countries know the name General Douglas MacArthur, one of the great warriors of all time. But he wrote this, and I'd like to end with this reading because I think it epitomized where we all want to be, the way we want to teach, the way we want to train, the way we want to develop our organizations and raise our children.

"Build me a son, O Lord, who will be strong enough to know when he is weak, and brave enough to face himself when he is afraid; one who will be proud and unbending in honest defeat, and yet humble and gentle in victory. Build me a son whose wishbone will not be where his backbone should be; a son who will know Thee and that to know himself is the foundation stone of knowledge. Lead him not, I pray, in the path of ease and comfort, but under the stress and spur of difficulties and challenge. Here let him learn to stand up in the storm; here let him learn compassion for those who fail.

Build me a son whose heart will be clean, whose goals will be high; a son who will master himself before he seeks to master other men; one who will learn to laugh, yet never forget how to weep; one who will reach into the future, and yet never forget the past. And after all these things are his, I pray, add enough of a sense of humor, so that he may always be serious, and yet never take himself too seriously. Give him humility, so that he may always remember the simplicity of true greatness, the open mind of true wisdom, and the meekness of true strength. Then I, his father, will dare to whisper, "I have not lived in vain."

You can see why I say that here is a warrior who left us a blueprint of what these old warriors were trying to teach us with what they defended, and that is that when we are free, when we are open, when we are ready to imagine it, to act on it, and to die for it, we will accomplish whatever we want to accomplish.

Marriage

Wedding Ceremony Written and Performed by Stan for His Granddaughter, Presley Whitehead and Her Husband Grayson

Dearly beloved families, your presence here today is very special to Presley and Grayson as they have limited the attendance to this small group of immediate family members. This places a unique responsibility on each of you as they look to us to support, bless, and celebrate this sacred occasion with them. They have chosen this spot where you are now sitting as the marital cathedral, where they will confirm their vows before God and with their families and with the spirit of great-grandparents, uncles, aunts, and brothers as witnesses. Chosen because it represents the unique valley where buffalo once roamed, the verdant meadows, wild grapes grew along the creeks and rivers and pioneers broke the virgin soil, bringing forth crops and civilization. This valley is a place they love, where they fell in love, and where they plan to fulfill their love and destiny. May you all remember and cherish this sacred ceremony, for on this day with love, we will forever bind Presley and Grayson as husband and wife.

Traditionally, this is the point where the minister asks, "Who gives this woman to this man?" And yet, Presley and Grayson have already given themselves to each other. So, today it seems more appropriate to ask both parents to stand and pledge their support to Presley and Grayson. So, I ask you now, "Do you pledge your love, support, and care to this union? Do you?" Instead of asking if anyone objects to this marriage, I now ask the family, "Do you pledge your love, support, and care to this union? Do you?"

Marriage is an ancient ritual practice by all civilizations. It is the result of man's need for love and companionship. An ancient Korean proverb says, "There is no winter without snow, there is no spring without sunshine, and there is no happiness without companionship." Jesus said, "For this reason, a man shall leave his mother and father and be joined to his wife, and they shall become one flesh." So no longer two, but one. Therefore, we solemnly bless this place and this event that consecrates the lives of Presley and Grayson from this day forward forever. Presley and Grayson, please face each other and hold hands under the leadership of God and before these witnesses. Presley Marie Whitehead, do you take Grayson Davies to be your lawfully wedded husband? By making this commitment, you are joining in the sacred covenant of marriage to Grayson. Do you promise to honor him in love to be sensitive to his needs, to comfort him in difficulty and to complete him as long as you both shall live?

Under the leadership of God and before these witnesses, do you Grayson Davies take Presley Marie Whitehead to be your lawfully wedded wife? By making this commitment, you are entering into the sacred covenant of marriage. Do you promise to honor her in love, to be sensitive to her needs, to comfort her in difficulty, and to put yourself beside her and complete her so long as you both shall live?

Exchanging wedding rings is a tradition that is over 5,000 years old. In the beginning, they were made of reeds, papyrus, leather, and eventually iron, and later precious metals such as silver and gold. Yet, no matter what they were made of, the symbol was the same. The round circle was continuous and never-ending, just like their love. The space inside symbolized the unknown and eternity which they would dwell together forever. Rings have been placed on different fingers. Yet, the most endearing has been the fourth finger of the left hand called in Ancient Rome, the Vena Amoris, or the vein of love, that runs from the finger to the heart.

Presley and Grayson have added new depth and meaning to this tradition by exchanging family heirlooms. Presley will give Grayson her great-grandfather's band. Mama Fred, her great-grandmother, was so proud of Grayson that a few months before she died, she asked them if they would honor her and Papa Fred by wearing his ring. Grayson will give Presley his grandmother's ring, which she designed using her first diamond she had worn as a young girl together with the emerald, she selected when creating the ring as a young woman. So, Grayson was thrilled this summer when she gave him this exquisite treasure to give to Presley.

One of the things that brought Presley and Grayson together was their love of wine. They work in the vineyard, they make wine, and they talk about it in the tasting room. It is an accepted fact that the best wines are blends of special varieties. Families are like that, people are like that, marriages are like that. So, we will watch as Grayson's wine is blended with Presley's wine. This blend will be good today, yet will be great tomorrow as this marriage between Presley and Grayson will get better with age.

By the power vested in me, by our mutual belief in God, by the state of Texas, I now pronounce you man and wife. You may kiss the bride.

Introduction of Hall of Fame Nominee, Pat Weir

We have now come to the point in our program where we will induct one of our industry's most distinguished leaders into the Direct Selling Hall of Fame. It is the highest honor the Direct Selling Association can bestow on an individual. Countries, cultures, and companies have always found it necessary to focus on these individuals whose dedication and service, sacrificial selflessness, and inspiring leadership have distinguished them from all the rest. The ancient Hebrews had their champions; France, its Legion of Merit; England, its knighthood; the US, the Congressional Medal of Honor; and the Direct Selling Association's equivalent, the Hall of Fame. As we emerge from direct selling's economic version of Desert Storm, we look around for our own hero to honor. It is not only tyrants that create heroes, but also the war against poverty, ignorance, and the stifling cynicism of socialism.

Therefore, we can be justifiably proud of our heroes, whose leadership in the industry creates jobs, wealth, and hope, making us a stronger people and a more whole nation. But like Desert Storm's hero, General Schwarzkopf, our heroes are not created in a blinding flash of brilliance, but from years of working in their trenches, always ready to go the extra mile to serve whenever possible. The Hall of Fame is symbolized by a crystal flame that stands two and a half feet tall. This artistic creation reminds us of the pure and indomitable spirit of today's inductee. The flame's light shines consistently in the same way our honoree has given service. The flame, suspended in time and space, will never go out, just as we will never forget the hard work, caring attitude, dedication, determination, and personal sacrifice that is being performed on our behalf.

The person we honor tonight is the epitome of this symbol. She has served this organization tirelessly for fourteen years, while at the same time moving from a position of security to president of one of our industry's largest companies, always making the industry a better place to work and serve America.

It is people, then, who change the world; not events, not machines, not technology. That may be why Leonard Bernstein said, "I love, honor, and adore people. I love them more than my race, religion, my national origin, or political persuasion. One person on the side of a mountain makes the entire mountain disappear for me." Tonight's hero has made a lot of mountains disappear for a lot of people. Many of us, who have worked closely with her for most of her DSA career, have been inspired, energized, and helped by her undaunted love of people.

It is a great moment in time for me to be part of this presentation, to see someone you respect and love, someone you count as a dear friend, be given our highest honor in the industry is an awesome event. Her work on the Executive Committee and Blueprint for Action Committee while I was chairman allowed me to know and see firsthand the power of her personality and strength of her character. Beginning as an annual meeting speaker, serving on the Finance Committee, influential on the Long-Range Planning Committee and leading us through some tough times as chairman of the board, are just a few more visible ways she has served this industry. The Executive Committee could not have made a better choice when they named this 1991 inductee into the Direct Selling Association's Hall of Fame, the president of Encyclopedia Britannica USA, Pat Weir.

To read more of Stan Fredrick's speeches and
learn about his legacy,please visit his website:

https://fredricklegacy.com